HADRIAN'S WALL

The National Trust Hadrian's Wall Estate

HADRIAN'S WALL
An Historic Landscape

Robert Woodside and
James Crow

The National Trust

First published 1999
by The National Trust
Reprinted 2000

ISBN 0-7078-0355-1

ISSN 0953-7163

British Library Cataloguing in Publication Data

A catalogue record for this book is available
from the British Library

Designed by James Shurmer

Printed in Great Britain by BAS Printers Ltd.

Front cover: Hadrian's Wall at Hotbank near
Housesteads with Crag Lough and Steel Rigg
beyond (NTPL/David Noton)

Back cover: View of the Sycamore Gap on the
Hadrian's Wall estate (NTPL/Paul Wakefield)

CONTENTS

COLOUR PLATES

TEXT FIGURES

PREFACE

Just over 150 years ago, the Newcastle solicitor and developer John Clayton began buying up parcels of land along the line of Hadrian's Wall. He had been alarmed that at a time of increasing archaeological interest in the Wall, the Roman remains were being quarried away for use in new farm buildings and drystone walls. An account of his life recalls that 'to talk of preserving the Wall was useless as long as well-shaped, handy-sized stones, lay ready to the hand of the farmer, and the carting away of stones went forward merrily' (Budge 1903, 6). Driven to act, in 1834 he bought up Steel Rigg and Hotbank farms, followed in 1838 by Housesteads Farm, Cawfields in 1844 and East Bog in 1848. He removed old farmsteads, many built of Roman stone, away from the line of the Wall and replaced them with handsome new farmhouses. He brought an end to damaging arable farming and introduced hardy breeds of cattle and sheep, as well as many other agricultural improvements, and he laid out plantations and shelterbelts around his farms, providing income as well as protection against the harsh Northumberland winds. By the 1870s, Clayton managed from his seat at Chesters an agricultural estate that stretched along the length of Hadrian's Wall from Great Chesters to Chollerford. Although it was run for profit, its real purpose was to conserve the archaeological remains within it. This was probably the first time that land had ever been deliberately purchased for the sole purpose of conservation anywhere in the world.

Things started to go wrong almost as soon as Clayton died in 1890. Despite F. G. Simpson's dedicated programme of excavation and conservation along the Wall, quarrying began at Cawfields in 1902, destroying some considerable archaeological remains. In 1930, following the break-up of the estate and the gift of Housesteads Fort to the National Trust, further quarrying was proposed all the way along the Whin Sill from Shield-on-the-Wall Farm to Housesteads Fort, effectively leaving the Wall suspended on a thin slice of rock. The quarrying could have meant jobs for 500 men at a time of deep depression, but conservation won out and in that year land at Housesteads Farm was given to the National Trust by one of its earliest benefactors, the historian G. M. Trevelyan of Wallington. Since then the Trust has acquired some 1,092.7 ha (2,700 acres) of land surrounding the Wall in what is arguably the most spectacular part of Northumberland. As successor to a significant part of the Clayton estate, the Trust has to balance conservation with the demands of modern agriculture and public access, and in so doing needs to know exactly just what it is conserving.

Hadrian's Wall is the best-known Roman monument in Britain. Running for 117.5 km (73 miles) between Bowness on Solway and Wallsend, it is testimony to the ingenuity and ambition of the Roman Empire. Whatever its purpose, be it frontier, custom post or symbol of the power of Rome, it has survived both physically and in the minds of subsequent generations who have lived on and studied its remains. To the post-Roman Britons it was a reminder of their imperial past, while to the Anglo-Saxons and Normans the Roman stone was a quarry for churches and castles. To medieval shepherds it was a shelter against cold winds and to the Elizabethans a symbol of England's struggle against the Scots. For the Border reivers it was a source of stone for their bastles, or fortified farmhouses, whilst for the Georgians it was a convenient route along which to align their Military Road to subdue the Jacobites. To the Victorians it was further evidence that Britain was the true successor to the power of the Roman Empire. In the twentieth century it has been glorified as an archaeological monument, set in a monumental landscape amongst clipped grass and interpretation boards, something frozen to be wondered at.

But Hadrian's Wall is a living landscape. The livelihoods of thousands depend on it: farmers, landowners, local business people, countryside managers, rangers and wardens, as well as archaeologists. It is visited by some 500,000 visitors every year, with over 150,000 to Housesteads Fort alone, and the story of the Roman wall is an educational resource for thousands of children from all over the country. However, archaeology is only part of the story, for this is an extraordinary geological land-scape, dominated by the Whin Sill and surrounded by some of the oldest rocks in England. The Roman remains themselves are home to lichens and lime-loving plants such as Springwort, and the loughs, or lakes, and mires are deservedly renowned as key-species habitats of high nature-conservation value. Birdlife plays an important role in the biodiversity of this Northumberland upland, with curlews often seen circling above the crags and crows crouching in the sparse woodlands. In every field are black-faced, hardy Northumberland ewes and shaggy Galloway cattle, all overseen by the farmer and his dogs. At any time of the year the sound of the wind can be deafening, relentlessly blowing in from all directions and echoing the vibrancy of life on the Wall.

Every kilometre of the Wall, from the mudflats of the Solway Forth to the final station at Segedunum in the shadow of the Swan Hunter Shipyard, has a tale to tell. Ours is focused on the Wall and the land either side of it between Cawfields and Sewingshields. Here Rome clearly left its hefty sandalprint on the landscape, but how many people know about the environmental deposits in Crag Lough or the Bronze Age standing stones at Cawfields? What of the tower house where Edward I stayed in 1307, the watchmen along the Crags in the sixteenth century, the bastle houses of the Border reivers or the scurrilous horse thieves at Housesteads and Busy Gap? Then there are the early farmsteads, many built of Roman stone, whose occupants struggled to eke out a living before agricultural improvement and enclosure were introduced at the end of the eighteenth century, together with limekilns, quarries, coalmines, and ironstone workings. Many may be surprised to learn that the landscape we know today probably owes more to the nineteenth than to the second or third centuries AD.

Whilst it is true to say that without Hadrian's Wall there would be no World Heritage Site, management in the twenty-first century must embrace all aspects of the landscape, from archaeology to nature conservation, public access to employment, good environmental practice to education. This process has already begun, but in the future there will be a number of difficult questions to resolve. Agricultural management along the Wall, for example, probably owes more to nineteenth century farming practices .than to any other time previously. Given the late twentieth-century crises in livestock farming, the question must be asked whether or not such practices are sustainable. If not, what are the alternatives? If this book has anything to say, then it is that radical changes in settlement and land use have happened in the past, often for the good as well as the bad. Future change, however, must be based on a full understanding of the whole environment.

But let's not forget for now what Hadrian's Wall is all about. Standing on the fort walls overlooking the bleak wastes north of Housesteads, one feels for the Roman legionary away from his family in Germany, Hungary or even in Syria. One imagines the chat in the communal latrines or over the wine and fish sauce in the *vicus* tavern, not to mention the patrols, square-bashing and perhaps even the occasional skirmish. 'Britunculi' ('little Britons'), 'Picts' or 'Scots' apart, the Wall must have been a hard and harsh posting. One cannot help but admire the brilliance and pig-headedness of the Roman mind – to build such an enormous feature is extraordinary enough, but to operate and maintain it for almost 300 years is just staggering. As Hadrian's Wall became Antonine's, then Severus's, then perhaps Constantine's and maybe even Arthur's Wall, both the landscape and the men and women living along it changed. As its use slipped out of memory, and its stones into people's backyards, it nevertheless still managed to retain its ability to inspire a sense of wonder. The rediscovery of the Wall in the eighteenth and its restoration in the nineteenth and twentieth centuries has ensured that the 500,000 or so visitors who come every year share in that wonder and will continue to do so for years to come.

ACKNOWLEDGEMENTS

This book is based on the results of two major surveys carried out on the National Trust estate between 1982 and 1995. The first was a measured survey at a scale of 1:1000 drawn up between 1982 and 1991 as part of the excavation programme directed by James Crow, assisted by Ralph Mills, Colin Lofthouse, Clive Waddington and students from the Department of Geomatics (formerly Surveying) at the University of Newcastle upon Tyne, who kindly loaned their equipment. The final drawings were prepared by Brian Williams.

The second survey, carried out by Robert Woodside between 1994 and 1995, sought to collate all available information so as to compile a Sites and Monuments database of every known archaeological and historic landscape feature on the estate. This was accompanied by an investigation into historic land use on the Trust property. The results of both surveys form the basis of this book.

Both authors would like to thank the Trust's archaeologists David Thackray, Philip Claris and Harry Beamish for their help and support. Thanks also to Professor Peter Salway, Academic Editor, and to the staff and post-graduate students of the Department of Archaeology, University of Newcastle upon Tyne, as well as the staff of the Archaeological Practice, Northumberland Record Office, English Heritage, Northumberland National Park, Northumberland County Council, The Royal Commission on the Historical Monuments of England and the Northumbria Region of the National Trust.

Particular thanks are due to the Trust's wardens Lawrence Hewer and Andrew Poad, as well as the estate tenants and their families, for their support and all those years of putting up with a stream of archaeologists.

1

A WALK ALONG THE WALL

We now quit the beautiful scenes of cultivation and enter upon the rude of nature and the wreck of antiquity.

(Hutton 1802)

Hadrian's Wall is one of the best-known archaeological remains in the British Isles. Originally built by the Roman Emperor Hadrian in about AD 130, it runs for 117.5 km (73 miles) from Wallsend in the east to Bowness-on-Solway in the west. It is a remarkable feat of Roman military engineering that consists not only of the Wall itself but also auxiliary forts, milecastles, turrets, roads, temporary camps, ditches and an enormous linear earthwork known as the Vallum, which runs parallel to the south of the Wall. Much of the Wall from Wallsend to Chollerford now lies under urbanisation and roads, but from there to Greenhead in Cumbria it can be clearly seen rising and falling along the line of the great Whin Sill, a large geological fault that cuts across much of northern England.

But this book is not just about Hadrian's Wall, or even the Romans, for that matter. It is about the 1,157.4 ha (2,860 acre) estate owned by the National Trust along the central 9.7 km (6 miles) of the Wall from Sewingshields to Cawfields, an often bleak but inspiring corner of Northumberland 9.7 km (6 miles) west of Hexham. It is about the land and how and why people came to live and work on this windswept and apparently barren moor. The archaeological evidence is certainly compelling and diverse. Starting in the Neolithic and continuing up to the present day, it tells a story of human settlement that is echoed all the way along the length of the Wall from Bowness to Wallsend.

At the heart of the Trust estate is Housesteads, deservedly known as one of the best-preserved Roman forts in Europe and today managed by English Heritage (Figure 1). In 1930, the fort and a length of the Wall from Milecastle 37 to the Knag Burn Gate was given to the nation, and since then the National Trust has striven to acquire land on either side of the Wall to ensure not only its protection, but also that of the remarkable upland landscape in which it is found. In this way, the Trust has followed in the footsteps of John Clayton, a Newcastle landowner and solicitor who established an archaeological park along much of the line of the Wall in the mid-nineteenth century. It is proper, therefore, that as successors to John Clayton, the National Trust calls its land on Hadrian's Wall an 'estate' (Figure 2).

Although Hadrian's Wall has been attracting the attention of antiquaries and

FIGURE 1 Housesteads Fort from the air. The fort and surrounding area presents one of the densest concentrations of archaeological sites in the country. The first antiquarian scholar to visit Housesteads was Christopher Hunter in 1702. (Photo: T. Gates, 1987 © copyright reserved)

archaeologists for almost 300 years, less is known of the other archaeological remains found along its length. We now realise that to ensure the continuing protection of the Wall, we must increase our understanding of the wider historic landscape in which it is set, and value it as much as the Roman remains themselves. The Trust estate is arguably the best place to begin this study, as both north and south of the Wall lies a diverse array of archaeological features, including standing stones, native settlements, medieval hamlets, bastle houses, farmsteads and farm-houses. It is peopled by saints, soldiers, Border reivers, farmers, antiquaries and archaeologists, all of whom have struggled to survive along the Wall or have worked hard to reveal its secrets. It is probably one of the greatest concentrations of archaeological remains in the north of England (a selective gazetteer of archaeological sites on the estate can be found at the end of the book).

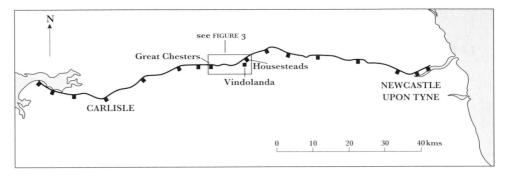

FIGURE 2 Location map.

A tour of the estate: from Sewingshields to Housesteads

While most visitors to Hadrian's Wall are familiar with Housesteads Fort, the rest of the Trust's estate is less well known and deserves to be explored. Travelling from east to west, Hadrian's Wall enters the estate about 1.6 km (1 mile) east of Housesteads Fort (Figure 3). Dominating the scene is the bold salient of Sewingshields Crags rising immediately to the east of Busy Gap. An ancient field bank forms the base for the field wall running north from the west end of the Crags and is part of the Black Dyke, a possible Bronze Age boundary running between the South and North Tyne, which now forms the eastern boundary of the estate. These Crags are the last major outcrop of the Whin Sill on the line of Hadrian's Wall. Here the Wall is inaccessible from the north because of the precipitous cliff and, uniquely, Milecastle 35 has no gate on the north side. Beyond Sewingshields Farm the Wall descends into Busy Gap, described in the sixteenth century as 'a goole passage and common entry of all thieves from Liddesdale and Gilsland'. 'Goole' has the same derivation as howl or ghoul in modern English, a word describing not just the raging of the wind, but the 'incourse' of thieves. A 'Busy Gap Rogue' was a term of abuse in sixteenth-century Newcastle reflecting the lawless life on the Anglo-Scottish border. The early nineteenth-century traveller, William Hutton, explained the name as 'So called from the frequency of the Picts and Scots breaking through this gap, and surprising the Romans and the Britons, and afterwards of the Moss Troopers'. Little disturbs the visitor today on what is now one of the least-visited lengths of the Wall, but to William Camden and his companion in 1599 this was the heart of outlaw country, as dangerous to the outsider and traveller as some of the less stable regions of the world are today.

Immediately to the north of Busy Gap is a triangular earthwork enclosure. This is clearly later than Hadrian's Wall, as the Wall-ditch forms the south side of what was probably a stock yard used in connection with droving cattle from the grazing further north down to the Tyne valley. Another triangular enclosure is known among the field banks to the north of Sewingshields Crags. Little of the Wall

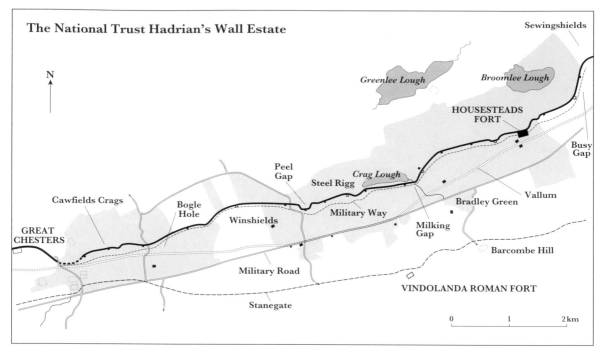

FIGURE 3 Map of the National Trust Hadrian's Wall estate. (R. Woodside)

survives to the east of Milecastle 35 along Kennel Crags, a name derived from the farm called Moss Kennels beside the Military Road. Milecastle 36 (King's Hill) occupies a very steep-sided location, with little access to the north, but over-looking Busy Gap to the east. To the east of Housesteads the Wall runs through the prominent valley of the Knag Burn, in which a gateway was constructed in the later second century. The Military Way, a road built in about AD 160 to link the forts along the Wall, swings around the south side of the wood to cross the burn just south of the gateway. This approach to the fort may predate the building of the Military Way, since an earlier road from Grindon and the Stanegate (the Roman cross-country route between Corbridge and Carlisle) can be seen on air photographs to join it a little to the east, representing the link to the earlier road system.

From Housesteads to Winshields

The estate hereon is dominated by the Whin Sill, the physical presence of which conditioned the route of Hadrian's frontier. Travelling west of Housesteads Fort the Wall line rises gently along Housesteads Crags and the scarp becomes steeper and more precipitous to the north. Milecastle 37 (Housesteads) was placed astride a narrow nick in the ridge top which allowed some access to the north, now in part obscured by nineteenth-century excavation spoil heaps. Westwards along the crags the slope levels off before the descent into the first major pass beyond Housesteads. Although this is amongst the most-photographed places on the Wall it remains the 'gap-with-no-name'. A length of the Wall-ditch survives in this gap, yet none is known in the gap besides Housesteads. The Wall then climbs a moderate slope on to Cuddy's Crags (a name said to derive from the Northumberland saint, St Cuthbert, known locally as 'Cuddy') and then descends into a narrow pass called Rapishaw Gap. Here there are clear traces of old trackways north and south of the Wall linking the well-preserved eighteenth- or nineteenth-century limekilns (structures used for burning limestone in order to produce lime for agricultural and other uses) (Figure 4); it is at this point also that the Pennine Way leaves the shelter of Hadrian's Wall and heads off north for its final leg towards Kirk Yetholm.

The Wall then follows one of the long crags, climbing to a height of 325 m, the highest point in the estate (Figure 5). It is named after the mid-eighteenth-century farm at Hotbank, an incongruous name in such an exposed place. In earlier documents it was referred to as 'Hodbank'. To the south of Hotbank are the farms of Bradley and Bradley Hall, a name which can be traced back to the early fourteenth century. It is likely that the Hotbank Crags were the location for the Bradley

FIGURE 4 View of Hadrian's Wall from the south. The Wall follows the crags on the skyline, whilst the Vallum follows the lower ground. The entire landscape is overlaid with a grid of late eighteenth-century drystone walls. (Photo: J. Crow, 1997)

Beacon, recorded in the sixteenth century at the time of the Border reivers. Hotbank Farm stands on the eastern edge of a wide pass now drained by the Bradley Burn, an outflow from the east end of Crag Lough, itself one of a group of shallow lakes or loughs (written in earlier documents as 'lowes'). The farmhouse is located on raised, dry ground, a position it shares with Milecastle 38 to the south. Immediately south of the Wall the Bradley Burn cuts through the Whin Sill at Milking Gap in a short but dramatic ravine. This gap, also known as Loughend, takes its name from the small structures used in the eighteenth and early nineteenth centuries as shelters for those milking cattle grazing on the rough pasture to the north of the wall. The shelters appear to be a later development of the seasonally occupied shielings – drystone-walled huts used by herdsmen in the Middle Ages. A milking house was found during the excavation of Milecastle 39 at Castle Nick, which seems also to have had the name of Milking Gap in the nineteenth century.

The earlier importance of this gap through the Whin Sill is shown by the late Iron Age and Roman-period settlement of Milking Gap, which lay south of the narrow gorge. Another settlement of similar date is situated on the hillside above Bradley Farm. Both settlements lay within the corridor formed by the Wall on the north and the Vallum to the south and it is unclear if they continued to be occupied after the building of the Wall. Normally this zone is very narrow, but from Housesteads to Great Chesters it is broad and a local compromise may have been reached with the local farmers allowing continued settlement.

Beyond Milking Gap the Whin Sill forms a bold scarp along Highshield and Peel

FIGURE 5 Hadrian's Wall on Hotbank Crags in 1907. Broomlee Lough can be seen in the distance. (Museum of Antiquities, University of Newcastle upon Tyne)

FIGURE 6 Relict boundaries and cultivation marks on Steel Rigg north of Hadrian's Wall. The earliest record of a farm here is in 1698, marking a significant transition in the way the landscape was used. (Photo: J. Crow, 1988)

Crags before the next wide pass at Steel Rigg. It is broken at the west end of Crag Lough by two nicks. Seen from the north they appear as a marked W in the otherwise unbroken north face of the crags. The eastern of these nicks is known as Sycamore Gap, a name of recent origin, derived from a solitary tree. In the nineteenth century it was referred to as Craighead. Before the next passage is a rocky, isolated hill known to archaeologists as Mons Fabricius, a name which recalls the visit in 1929 of one of the century's most eminent scholars of Roman frontier studies, Professor Ernst Fabricius. Sheltering behind the Wall at this point are the remains of three shielings, seasonally occupied by the inhabitants of the Tyne valley during the Middle Ages. Below this hill to the west is the slightly broader gap of Castle Nick, the name deriving from the visible remains of Milecastle 39. John Hodgson, the nineteenth-century historian, gave this gap another local name, 'The Door'.

The line of the Peel Crags continues as far as Peel Gap, interrupted only by a narrow rocky defile called Cat Stairs, a name also used for a similar gap in the Whin Sill east of Milecastle 35 on Sewingshields Crags. Throughout this length from Milking Gap westwards, the crags present a formidable barrier with the additional deterrent of Crag Lough (and other lakes beyond Castle Nick now drained), yet the line of the Roman wall continues, rising and falling across the steep nicks. The descent into Peel Gap is one of the most precipitous along the entire line. This gap is another overflow channel and Roman and modern culverts allow the ground to the north to drain across the Wall. 'Peel' is the name used for the crags, the gap and the cottage to the south, all deriving from what is possibly a medieval tower located on the south side of the Wall. North of the crags lie the remains of a late seventeenth-century farmstead and its associated enclosures, known from documentary evidence to have been called Steel Rigg (Figure 6). This farm was replaced by another farmhouse of the same name which occupied the site of the modern car-park until removed in the mid-nineteenth century. The name 'Steel' is fairly common in Northumberland and describes a steep-sided ridge, which here runs eastwards almost as far as Crag Lough, parallel to the Wall and crags.

From Winshields to Cawfields

The wide pass of Steel Rigg climbs easily towards Winshields and the site of Milecastle 40, just outside the National Trust estate. The Wall-ditch runs from the bottom of Peel Gap as far as the milecastle, but it appears as if the westernmost end was unfinished just short of Milecastle 40. The summit of Winshields beyond is the highest point of the Wall at 345 m, with some of the most desolate scenery as far as Melkridge Common. To the south-east of the summit, like miniature canyons, are the steep-sided valleys of Green Slack, which provide no passage across the Whin Sill. The next gap is called Lodhams Slack and is broad enough to be defended by the Wall-ditch. From there the whinstone ridge re-enters the estate, crossing Melkridge Common towards the site of Milecastle 41. This milecastle is often referred to as Shield-on-the-Wall, after the farmstead which occupied its site until the middle of the nineteenth century. The stock-yard wall can still be traced as well as the outline of the milecastle. A large building block with a typically Roman lewis-hole (a hole at the top of a stone used for lifting), one of the voussoirs from the milecastle gate, was rebuilt in the field wall to the east. The farm was moved south of Caw Gap and the new farmhouse shares similar architectural details with the farmhouse at Housesteads built by John Clayton in c.1860. The remains of a small bell pit, part of the nineteenth-century coalmining operation in the area, can be seen just south of the farmhouse.

Just beyond Milecastle 41 is the ominously named Bogle Hole, which contains the remains of a neatly set-out line of shielings. 'Bogle' means 'ghost' or 'spirit' in the local Northumberland dialect, and this spot is said to be associated with a number of folktales, although none, sadly, has ever been recorded. Beyond the Bogle Hole the land drops steeply to meet another gap in the Whin Sill, on the east side of which are the remains of another post-medieval farmhouse removed by John Clayton in the 1860s. From here Hadrian's Wall stretches along the top of Cawfields Crags for over 1.5 km (1 mile), culminating at Milecastle 42, the first milecastle along the wall to be properly excavated by Clayton in 1852. The Wall was quarried away beyond the milecastle at the turn of this century, but not before it was recorded by F. G. Simpson in 1909 (Simpson, G. 1976). On Cawfields Common

FIGURE 7 Cawfields Common from the air facing north. Here the parallel lines of the Wall, Military Way, Vallum, Stanegate and the Military Road are joined by the remains of Roman temporary camps, prehistoric cord rig, nineteenth-century ironstone working and twentieth-century whinstone quarrying. Cawfields Common is possibly the most archaeologically 'intense' place in Northumberland. Milecastle 42, Great Chesters Roman fort and three other temporary camps lie just outside the photograph. The protection of Cawfields Common is vital to ensure not only the survival of the archaeology, but also the livelihoods of those who live on or near the Wall. (T. Gates, 1992 © copyright reserved)

is the most remarkable length of the Vallum along the entire stretch of Hadrian's Wall (Figure 7). Running unbroken for over 1.6 km (1 mile), it bears evidence of a number of phases of cutting and filling. Two Bronze Age standing stones known as the Mare and Foal can be seen in the south-east corner of this field, although there may have been as many as three or four stones here originally. The Stanegate, the Roman road that originally formed the northern limits of the empire, enters the National Trust's property at this point, but has been greatly disturbed by later quarrying. A small patch of prehistoric cord-rig ploughing, a narrow form of ridge and furrow, has also been identified here.

On either side of the Haltwhistle Burn are the remains of as many as seven Roman temporary marching camps, some of which may have been practice camps thrown up by the army before campaigning to the north. Others may have been occupied whilst the Wall was being built. On the west side of the Haltwhistle Burn is a small permanent fort, constructed to protect the Stanegate as it passed between Vindolanda (Chesterholm) and Magna (Carvoran). It is likely that the fort went out of use shortly before or after the completion of the fort at Great Chesters. Aerial photographs have revealed that this land was heavily cultivated in the post-medieval period, and the remains of narrow ridge and furrow cultivation can be traced on the ground. Running alongside the Haltwhistle Burn is a disused tramway that once carried whinstone from Cawfields Quarry down to Haltwhistle and the industries of the South Tyne valley.

Conclusion

This tour along the top of the Wall shows the enormous diversity of archaeological activity in this small area of Northumberland. It is a pattern that can be followed along the entire length of Hadrian's Wall outside the urban centres of Newcastle and Carlisle. The scope of this book may be restricted by the boundaries of the National Trust's estate, but it draws in a number of examples from throughout the north of England. It is not, however, intended to be a study of the setting of the whole length of the Wall, but only the part from Sewingshields to Cawfields that makes up the Trust's estate. By studying how this particular part of the landscape was developed, however, it should be possible to gain a greater understanding of the entire setting of Hadrian's Wall as it is known today.

2

THE PREHISTORIC LANDSCAPE

The origins of the landscape

The Hadrian's Wall estate is dominated by the Whin Sill, a jagged line of rock that forms one of the most remarkable landscapes in the British Isles (Figure 8). It is also noted for its Carboniferous rocks, glacial loughs (lakes) and boggy Border mires. The earliest rocks on the estate were laid down during the Lower Carboniferous period, approximately 320 million years ago, while Northumberland lay beneath the ocean at the mouth of a great river which flowed through a landmass to the north-east. The river delta, which spread over most of the north of England, was responsible for the deposition of much of the geological strata in the area of the estate. These sediments were made up of layers of limestone, mudstone and sandstone. The sandstone is typically medium/coarse-grained, cross-bedded and micaceous, and has been known to contain seatearth, a good indicator of conditions found at the mouths of great rivers. The duration of such open-sea conditions is reflected by the varying thickness of limestone. These periods of deposition were invariably terminated by the encroachment of alluvial detritus brought down by the river, when shale was overlaid by sandstone. Repetition of such conditions led to the formation of layers of sedimentary deposits, the most notable exposures being found around Bradley Farm and Broomlee Lough. One of the units found running to the north of Broomlee Lough is particularly noteworthy: this is Oxford Limestone, which has a high fossil content including Crinoids and shell fragments, and was later used by the Romans for making lime mortar (Buckley 1972, 20).

Around 295 million years ago geological faulting caused a band of ancient quartz dolorite, known as whinstone, to force itself through the later deposits of sandstone and limestone (Fitch and Miller 1967). The result was the formation of the Whin Sill, a formidable outcrop of rock that runs across the country from Teesdale, northwards to the Tyne Gap and then across Northumberland to the coast at Alnmouth with isolated stretches on the Farne Islands. Between the Tipalt Burn, near the Northumberland and Cumbrian border, and Sewingshields Crags, the Whin Sill presents in many places a bold, often sheer, face towards the north, reaching its greatest height on Winshields Crags at 345 m. The best exposure is on the southern banks of Crag Lough (Figure 9), where it rises up as magnificent northward-facing crags backed by long slopes falling away towards the South Tyne at a dip of approximately 25 degrees (Buckley 1972, 20). It is particularly well

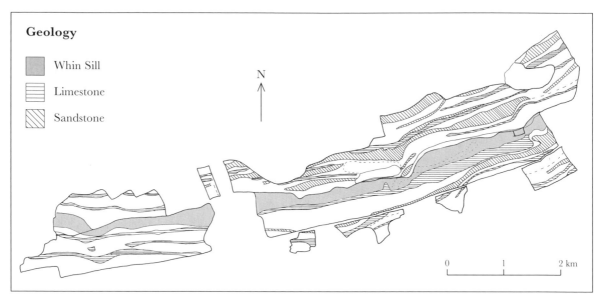

FIGURE 8 Simplified map of the geology on the National Trust Hadrian's Wall estate. (R. Woodside)

jointed and badly weathered in places, forming a considerable obstacle to movement north and south. In the early eighteenth century it was described as a 'vast and horrid steepness of rocks to the north', and its presence has had an enormous influence over human activity since prehistory. The name derives from the local word 'whin', meaning 'hard', and 'sill', another local term used to describe a flat bed of rock (Fortley 1993, 142).

Along the whole length of the Sill are a number of 'nicks' or 'gaps' which developed along joint planes caused by localised faulting. The nicks were developed further by the overflow channels of ice-dammed lakes which temporarily existed during the last stage of the Ice Age, around 12,000 years ago. These glacial overflow streams cut through the Sill as they moved southwards, creating steep-sided nicks at places such as Caw Gap, Peel Gap, and Castle Nick. Some overflow channels formed broader valleys, such as the Knag Burn below Housesteads Fort, which allowed easy passage. Another legacy of the last glaciation are the three small loughs to the north of the Whin Sill, which were formed by ice scooping out soft shale bands to leave cavities that later filled with water. One of these lakes, Crag Lough, lies at the foot of Highshield Crags and feeds the Bradley Burn. To the north-east of Housesteads is lonely Broomlee Lough, its shores forming part of the boundary of the estate, the bottom of which consists of limestone and sandstone beds, with the sandstone of Dove Crags jutting out above the south-east side of the lake. The third, Greenlee Lough, is the largest of the three and feeds the Caw Burn which, with its outcrops of sandstones, shales and limestones, marks the westernmost boundary of the estate. These loughs are

FIGURE 9 The Whin Sill at Peel Crags forming a formidable barrier to the north. The land at the bottom of the crags is often boggy. Crag Lough is one of the surviving glacial lakes that formed to the north of the crags in the post-Devensian period. (Museum of Antiquities, University of Newcastle upon Tyne)

the only remnant of a wider pattern of lakes, still present in the eighteenth century, but since drained.

The glaciations that formed the loughs were also responsible for the deposition of loamy sand and clay that lies across the estate to a thickness of between 3 and 6 m. It is at its most fertile and easily cultivated at Housesteads Farm. Boggy and peaty ground formed wetlands known as the Border Mires, which were once widespread across this part of Northumberland, but are now greatly reduced due to extensive drainage over the last 150 years. Some of the mires still survive, however, between the line of the Vallum and the slope of the Whin Sill at East and West Bog Farms, and boggy ground is still to be found around the shores of the loughs.

The earliest settlements

The end of the last Ice Age in Britain was a period that saw an improvement in the climate and the domination of birch and alder forest across the northern uplands. By c.6500 BC, the land bridge that had joined Britain to Europe was lost beneath rising sea levels, after which evidence of human activity increases throughout Britain. Archaeological evidence for Early Mesolithic settlement in Northumberland, or, indeed, for most of northern England and Scotland, is minimal (Burgess 1984, 127). It is not until the Late Mesolithic that there is an increase in activity along the coastal plain and along the three great river systems that flow eastwards from the Pennines, the Tyne, the Wear and the Tees. The river sites often occupied terraces or bluffs above the main river or tributary, for example on opposite sides of the Tyne at Gallowhill Farm, Corbridge, and Low Shilford, Riding Mill. Evidence has been found for Mesolithic activity in Tynedale to a height of 500 m, showing that the uplands were explored at this time. Investigation of sites such as Star Carr in North Yorkshire suggests that human activity during the Mesolithic was limited to hunting and gathering in marginal areas (Higham, 1986). During the winter, hunting groups, made up of small- or extended-family units, would have settled in the lowlands, moving on to the uplands in the summer to follow the red deer. Occupation sites, therefore, would only have been in use for part of the year before the hunting groups moved on. Limited woodland clearance may also have occurred at the end of the Late Mesolithic, indicating early stock control (Burgess 1984, 131). There is, however, no direct archaeological evidence for Mesolithic activity on the Hadrian's Wall estate, although the upland nature of the land above the Tyne valley may have meant that it was at some time visited by the migrating deer, followed closely by groups of hunters.

The first farmers reached Britain between 5000 and 4000 BC, and there is increasing evidence for settlement in the north coinciding with a decline in elm, carbon dated to between 3500 and 3000 BC. The earliest evidence for human activity on the Hadrian's Wall estate comes from a palaeobotanical study of the ancient botanical and environmental remains conducted by Newcastle University in 1992 on deposits taken from Crag Lough. This revealed a decline in elm coinciding with an increase in grass pollens, plantains (*Plantago lanceolat* and *Plantago major*), and a peak in corn buttercup (*Ranunculus*), genera typical of open fields, trackways, and other areas of deliberate clearance and disturbance. The tree cover was reduced but hazel was maintained and coppiced for stakes and fruit. The absence of cereal pollen (large *Gramineae*) would suggest pastoral activity rather than arable land-use, with domesticated or semi-domesticated animals grazing in woodland clearings. This period of human settlement seems to have been short-lived, however, as the palaeo botanical evidence from Crag Lough reveals a decline in anthropogenic indicator species (plantains, grasses, etc), corresponding to a reciprocal increase in birch levels, suggesting that pastoral activity occurred and then dropped off relatively quickly.

Large-scale clearances of woodland in the upland areas of Britain are known to date from about 2500 BC (Pearson 1993, 99). Evidence from Crag Lough reveals a sharp decline in alder and other arboreal pollens and an increase in grass pollen. Once the woodland had been cleared, upland mull soils tended to be lost by leaching and erosion and it was difficult for trees to regenerate. As a result, woodland was generally replaced by grassland, heath and peat. Arable cultivation seems to have been introduced at this time and the presence of cereal pollen and a peak in the levels of cornfield weed suggests that a rotational system of ley (slash-and-burn) farming, whereby cultivation is alternated with fallow (which usually reverted to woodland), may have been in operation. Rackham, however, observed that British woodland 'burns like wet asbestos', suggesting that slash-and-burn cultivation would have been unlikely (1986, 72).

The evidence of forest clearing, pastoralism and limited arable cultivation may suggest the presence of a settlement in the vicinity, although none has as yet been identified. Physical evidence for Neolithic settlement, however, with the exception of a few chance finds of hand-axes, is particularly sparse on land above 250m, and noticeably so in the Cheviot Hills and to the north of Hadrian's Wall towards Thrunton Crags and the Simonside Hills. Neolithic settlement seems to have been concentrated largely in the lowlands and valleys of Northumberland, most notably in the Millfield Basin near Wooler. Hand-axe and pottery distribution, together with burial practices and the growth of 'public' monuments, such as henges, would suggest a complicated social and political fabric (Burgess 1984, 138).

The second millennium BC

At some time in the early second millennium BC there was a considerable shift in settlement patterns away from low-lying sites, such as the Millfield Plain, towards the occupation of more upland sites. The growth in the number of large public monuments across previously fertile and well-cultivated soil may indicate an increase in land division caused by the demands of a growing population. It is at this time that the exploitation of the uplands is marked by the erection of monolithic structures, such as standing stones. The most prominent monument thought to date

FIGURE 10 The Mare and Foal standing stones. These are the earliest extant evidence for human activity on the National Trust Hadrian's Wall estate, although their function is not fully understood. (Photo: J. Crow, 1997)

to the second millennium BC on the Hadrian's Wall estate is the Mare and Foal stone circle at Cawfields Farm (Figure 10). The original circle may have been 5 m in diameter, but only two stones now remain standing of the three shown on the 1769 Armstrong map of Northumberland. It has been suggested that there may once have been four stones set in a square, a feature known as a 'four-poster', similar to that at Goat Stones on the North Tyne. The newly discovered stone circle at Gibb's Hill just north of the estate and the stone circle to the north-east up the Caw Burn, south of Greenlee Lough, indicate a spread of Bronze Age occupation throughout the area, although it has been suggested that the Greenlee Lough circle may have been a cairn (Welfare 1986, 35). The purpose of these particular stones is uncertain but, whether religious or astronomical, they would certainly have served

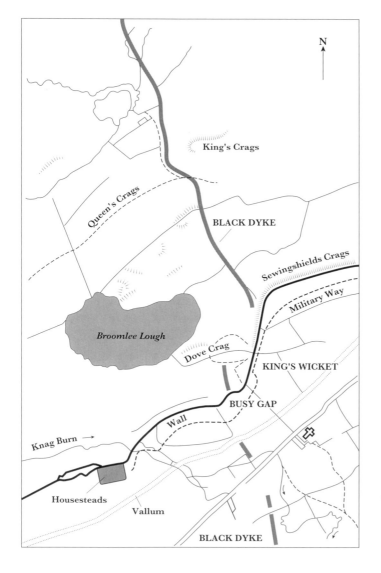

FIGURE 11
The line of the Black Dyke north of Hadrian's Wall. (After Spain 1921)

as a focal point for the communities in the region. Possible cairns at Milking Gap and Hotbank Farm may similarly date to this period and have acted as territorial markers at this important passage through the Whin Sill.

Further evidence for Bronze Age activity has been recorded at Sycamore Gap, where a stone boundary can be seen running south from the gap and into the mire, where it disappears. The line of the wall is cut by a Roman road. In 1987, a sample of soil taken from along the line of the boulder wall by Judy Turner of Durham University revealed that the wall was overlaid by the mire, which contained Bronze Age deposits dating back to the second millennium BC. The line of the boulder wall reappears running east to west along the bottom of the south slope of Peel Crags, revealed when the modern track leading to Sycamore Gap was built in 1982. Another boulder wall was identified by Clive Waddington in 1993 running along the bottom of Kennel Crags from King's Wicket to the Knag Burn. The boulder wall was truncated by the wall-ditch, and so is certainly prehistoric, and survives to a width of up to 1 m. Unfortunately, it has been heavily disturbed by modern field drainage. The purpose of these boulder walls is uncertain, but it has been suggested that they served to demarcate territory between tribal areas. The fact that they follow the line of the Whin Sill, a not inconsiderable natural boundary in itself, suggests that the boundaries were symbolic, re-establishing earlier divisions. Another demarcation of land is the Black Dyke, a linear earthwork with a ditch on the west side that runs between the South Tyne and the North Tyne and is best seen between Sewingshields Crags and Queen's Crags, where it forms the eastern boundary of the estate (Figure 11). The purpose of the dyke is unknown. It is presumed to be prehistoric but its relationship with the Vallum is unclear. Local tradition recalls that it formed the boundary between the Anglo-Saxon kingdom of Bernicia and the native British kingdom of Rheged using the prehistoric dyke as a demarcation rather than a defensive barrier, although there is no evidence for this (Spain 1921). The presence of mixed agriculture, stone circles and linear boundaries between farming communities suggests a widespread hierarchical community centred along the line of the Whin Sill.

The late Bronze Age saw an intensification in agriculture with significant woodland clearance and both pastoral and arable farming in operation. Settlement in the region was characterised by open, unenclosed farmsteads, such as Green Knowe in Peebleshire and Hallshill near Steng Moss in Redesdale, Northumberland (Higham 1986, 85, 87). However, climatic deterioration between 1200 and 800 BC led to the abandonment of exposed upland areas as an increase in levels of soil wash reduced poorly drained areas to impoverished moorland or blanket peat. Expansion and settlement in upland and marginal regions became impossible and pressures on available land led to 'depopulation, mutual aggression and pauperization' (Higham 1986, 117). A greatly depleted population established new settlements in the lowlands and valleys and the uplands were given over to hunting and grazing. Palaeobotanical evidence from Crag Lough reveals some re-establishment of mixed deciduous woodland at this time. During the tenth to seventh centuries BC the population recovered and edged back towards its former numbers, only to be reduced by further climatic deterioration in the late seventh and sixth centuries BC (Burgess 1984, 161).

The first millennium BC

The pressure on land brought about an increasing awareness of territory and the need for protection from encroachment or outright attack from neighbouring groups. Settlements in the uplands began to be defended, initially by a single palisade, but this was later superseded by new earthwork defences. Hill-forts, known in Northumberland from the fifth century BC, began to dominate the land-scape, and, although they are much less common in the south-west of the county, two examples are known from just outside the National Trust estate at Barcombe Hill and Greenlee Lough. Barcombe Hill is a univallate (single-banked) hill-fort with a ditch on the south side, later occupied by a Roman signal station (Figure 12). Greenlee Lough is similarly univallate, although semicircular in form due to the crags, and encloses an Iron Age settlement (Welfare 1986, 35). The origins of both these sites are unknown; it would seem that the deterioration in the climate brought about a crisis that led to the collapse of a number of social institutions as well as to a decline in metalware and pottery production. Excavations of a palisaded enclosure on Fenton Hill above the Millfield Plain provided a date of between c.880 and 760 BC for the earliest phase of defences (Burgess 1984, 157). Other sites have provided later dates for the earliest phase of defence, mostly in the sixth or seventh centuries BC. The movement into the uplands and less favourable soil areas may suggest competition for the more fertile lowland zones and the development of larger tribal units. As the millennium progressed, so the enclosures became more heavily defended, with larger earthwork palisades and ditches, leading to a peak in hill-fort construction, probably in the fifth century BC. Some 150 hill-forts and defended settlements are known throughout Northumberland, such as Harehaugh and Yeavering Bell in the Cheviot Hills.

Before the Romans

When the hill-fort sites were eventually abandoned is not fully understood, but there seems to have been a shift towards more open forms of settlement in the last two centuries before the Roman invasion. The late prehistoric period saw an expansion of agricultural settlement into the uplands and extensive woodland clearing has been dated to AD 20 ± 60 at Steng Moss and AD 2 ± 45 at Fellend Moss, both in Northumberland. Rectilinear farmsteads containing hut circles and enclo-sures, such as those at Milking Gap and north of Bradley Farm (Figure 13), are known from this period. It was long believed that stone-built enclosures were

FIGURE 12 Barcombe Hill Iron Age fort lies just off the National Trust Hadrian's Wall estate, but overlooks one of the most important routes between the Tyne valley and the uplands beyond. The landscape is scarred by the remains of later cultivation and industry. (Photo: T. Gates, 1987 © copyright reserved)

3
ROME'S SANDALPRINT

We now enter this city of the dead. All is silent; but dead indeed to all human sympathies must be the soul of that man who, in each broken column, each turf-covered mound, each deserted hall, does not recognise a voice telling him, trumpet-tongued, of the rise and fall of empires, of the doom and ultimate destiny of man!

(Bruce 1881, 142)

The Roman invasion

In AD 43 the Emperor Claudius, in need of a military victory, invaded Britain and began more than three and a half centuries of Roman occupation. Within thirty years southern England had been absorbed into the Empire and was well on the way towards adopting Roman culture; in the north, the armies consolidated their conquests with forts and roads. In AD 78 a new governor, Agricola, pushed into Scotland, creating a fort at Corbridge as a supply base and establishing permanent forts throughout the lowlands. Demands for more troops from elsewhere in the Empire eventually led to the withdrawal of the army from Scotland. More permanent forts were built at Corbridge and Carlisle as the far north was gradually abandoned.

The Roman withdrawals from Scotland (AD 80–105) heightened the importance of the Tyne–Solway isthmus and the cross-country route between Corbridge and Carlisle known as the Stanegate (Figure 14). It seems that new military posts were added to the line of the road to accommodate some of the withdrawing troops. The exact date of the establishment of these posts is uncertain but they probably date to the early second century AD as Trajan consolidated the strategic position of the Stanegate. One of these new installations was the small fort or fortlet on the Haltwhistle Burn, and another at Throp west of Carvoran. The Haltwhistle Burn fortlet was only 64 m by 52 m in size, with earthen ramparts later given a stone facing. It lay within an irregular ditch and contained at least one barrack building, together with a centurion's quarters, a store and a part-walled yard, as well as an administrative building. The fortlet overlooks the Stanegate as it passes through a vulnerable crossing over the burn. Whether the Stanegate actually formed the frontier of the Roman province at this time is uncertain, but it would seem that the position of the forts on the road influenced later decisions to establish a linear barrier across northern Britain.

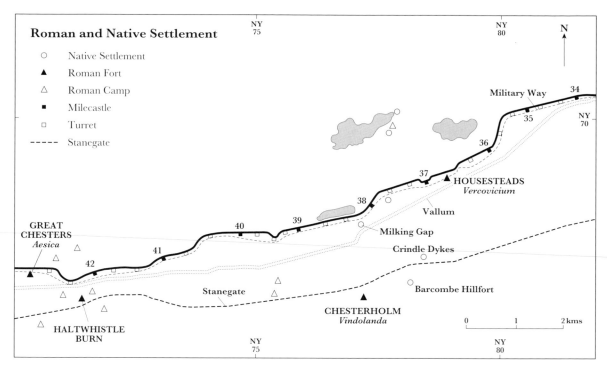

Roman and Native Settlement

- ○   Native Settlement
- ▲   Roman Fort
- △   Roman Camp
- ■   Milecastle
- □   Turret
- -----   Stanegate

Military Way   34

35

NY 70

36

37

▲ **HOUSESTEADS**
Vercovicium

Vallum

38

GREAT CHESTERS *Aesica*

40

39

Milking Gap

41

Crindle Dykes

42

Stanegate

Barcombe Hillfort

CHESTERHOLM *Vindolanda*

HALTWHISTLE BURN

NY 75   NY 80

0   1   2 kms

FIGURE 14 Native and Roman settlement on the National Trust Hadrian's Wall estate.

The building of the Wall

In AD 117 Hadrian became emperor and, contrary to his predecessor Trajan's expansionist policies, began to consolidate the boundaries of the Empire. In AD 122 he visited Britain and ordered a wall to be built which, according to a later source, would 'divide Roman from barbarian'. The longest visible length of Hadrian's Wall is in Cumbria from Milecastle 48 (Poltross Burn) to Birdoswald Fort, including the crossing of the River Irthing at Willowford. But the history of the structure of the Wall, its turrets and milecastles is best known in the neighbourhood of Housesteads, from Sewingshields in the east to Winshields in the west. Most of the Cumbrian sector was exposed by the Ministry of Works during the 1950s, but with only limited archaeological supervision. By contrast, the Housesteads sector of the Wall, although much was disinterred and restored by John Clayton in the nineteenth century, has seen the most intensive investigations this century, first by F. G. Simpson for the Chesters estate immediately before the First World War (Figure 15) (Simpson, G. 1976), and later on Sewingshields milecastle and Crags in the late 1970s and in the National Trust's estate, between Steel Rigg and Housesteads, in the 1980s. As a result more is known about this sector of Hadrian's Wall than any other. The extent of our knowledge could be misleading for the study of Hadrian's Wall as a whole, since in the 13 km (8 miles) of the middle lengths

FIGURE 15 Peel Crags Turret (39a) from the east, seen during F. G. Simpson's excavations in 1911. The later blocking of the turret recess is clearly visible. Today the turret walls can be barely discerned in the turf. (F. G. Simpson)

not only is the topography very different from the rolling hills to east and west, but the available building resources also differ as do the tactical needs of the barrier. None the less it is worth reviewing what has been learnt as part of the whole Wall line.

Broad Wall and Narrow Wall

The earliest phase of the building of the Wall was the construction of milecastles and turrets, linked by the laying-out of the foundations, built to a width of 3.5 m, known as the Broad Wall (Crow 1989). Most of the turrets between milecastles 34 and 40 are known to have been constructed first with wing-walls (side walls) to receive the adjacent Roman wall. At some point in the early construction of the Wall it was decided to reduce its thickness from 3.5 m to 2.3 m, the narrower wall being superimposed on the broader footings. Evidence for a change in construction can be seen at Turret 39a on Peel Crags, where there are no known wing-walls and the turret appears to have been constructed to the slightly later Narrow Wall width. If the turret system was incomplete at this stage in the construction of the Wall, the same can be observed for the milecastles. At Milecastle 37, west of Housesteads, for example, the north gate and foundations of the south gate were constructed to the Broad Wall specifications of 3.5 m, whilst the north curtain and the side walls were constructed later to Narrow Wall dimensions. Similar breaks in the construction sequence can be seen at Milecastle 38 (Hotbank) and further west at Milecastle

42 (Cawfields). Milecastles 39 (Castle Nick) and 40 (Winshields), west of Hotbank, seem not to have been constructed at all before the building of the Narrow Wall. At Castle Nick, the gap in the Whin Sill scarp was partly filled by a single broad foundation, 3.6 m in width. This was more substantial than usually survives and seems to have been always intended as the footing for a gate, but neither the north or south gates of this milecastle were constructed until the Narrow Wall phase. Less is known from the next milecastle, Winshields (40), which appears to be located at the extreme west end of a continuous length of Broad Wall and ditch terminating at the east side of Peel Gap. The gates and walls of the milecastle as excavated were also of Narrow Wall phase.

Even less can be deduced about the early phases of Milecastle 35 (Sewingshields), because there was never a gate on the north side above the precipice, and the south gateway was completely robbed away in the Middle Ages. There was good evidence for the Broad Wall phase, both below the north side of the milecastle and along the Sewingshields Crags to the west. Although only intermittent lengths are known in detail, the Broad Wall was continuous along the Crags. Traces of it are next seen in the valley of the Knag Burn and running continuously westwards below the fort, where it is visible at Turret 36b. A further section can be seen at the foot of the north curtain of Milecastle 37. Limited excavation revealed further traces in Milking Gap, north of the field wall, and on Highshield Crags. On the steep descents, where there is little or no soil over the bedrock, little trace survives, but it is clear that in some places the later Narrow Wall was constructed at a different alignment to that of the first foundation.

Up to Sycamore Gap the line of the Broad Wall was apparently continuous in the gaps and on the crags of the Whin Sill. From here onwards it was restricted to the gaps alone. One exception is a small isolated length on the top of the isolated hill known as Mons Fabricius. This is independent of the later wall and appears to have been ignored by the later phase of wall builders, who chose a slightly easier route on the edge of the hill. The reason for this change is unclear, but from here on the Broad Foundation was only constructed in wide gaps in the Whin Sill such as Peel Gap and Steel Rigg or between Cawfields and Great Chesters (Figure 16). The continuous line of foundations does not resume until west of Carvoran up to the crossing of the Irthing.

One question that this incomplete line raises is to what extent it was left as a foundation of large whinstone blocks no more than two courses high, or whether in some places the Wall was at least built up to several courses in height before the narrower work replaced it. One of the difficulties the Roman builders faced in the middle lengths of the Wall was that there was no sandstone immediately available for its construction. The whinstone of the crags was to hand, but needed skilful knapping to be used as a facing-stone. Invariably the Broad Wall consists of large, rough whinstone blocks with a core of soil and rubble. At Peel Gap, however, where the earliest phase of the Wall was partly covered by peat and other

FIGURE 16 Hadrian's Wall at the east end of Peel Gap. The three main phases of the Wall can be seen: the Broad Wall foundations, the Narrow Wall built during Hadrian's reign and the extra-narrow wall constructed after AD 200 with hard white mortar. (Photo: J. Crow, 1986)

vegetation connected with a large primary culvert through the Wall, the survival of several sandstone facing-blocks shows that construction above the footings had started before the Narrow Wall was begun. Elsewhere it might be argued that the sandstone blocks were reused in the later Narrow Wall, but there remains the puzzling feature of so much of the Broad Wall where the footings were not reused.

The first culvert at Peel Gap was built for the Broad Wall and was allowed to silt up and almost disappear before the construction of the Narrow Wall. How long this process took is not clear, although archaeological evidence suggests that it is likely to have been more than a couple of winters. Why the work on the Broad Wall was abandoned is normally explained by the construction of the forts such as Housesteads and Great Chesters along the line. Yet at this stage the Wall could not have been more than an overgrown building site with only some of its installations completed. In no sense could it divide the Romans from the Barbarians (Crow 1995).

When work resumed on the Wall itself it was constructed entirely to Narrow Wall specifications, mostly of sandstone facing-stones on footings of whinstone. The core of the Narrow Wall was of whin rubble with little or no mortar and only the facings were pointed. The height of this wall can be estimated from the archway surviving at Milecastle 37 to have been at least 4.5 m. On the north face there was a chamfered string course (a slightly projecting line of stones in which the sides of individual stones had been cut away at an angle), probably at the junction of the top of the curtain and the base of the parapet. Many hundreds of these chamfered blocks have been found in the course of excavations on Hadrian's Wall, invariably on the north side, and they provide the only positive proof that the Wall had a parapet (Figure 17). It is less certain whether there was a wall-walk at the top, but the presence of a parapet makes this likely. There is, however, little evidence to suggest that the parapet had crenellations with merlons (jagged upstanding fortifications), even if they are shown on the famous Rudge Cup (Johnson 1989, 42). Merlons can be demonstrated at the forts, milecastles and at turrets from surviving capstones, but the latter have not been found on the line of the wall. How the wall-walk was surfaced is also not known. Several flat stones suitable for paving have been found, but not in sufficient numbers to clearly demonstrate how the wall-top was finished off and protected from water percolating through the wall-core.

The gates at Milecastle 39 (Castle Nick) were built in the Narrow Wall phase and were less substantial than at the milecastles immediately to the east, Hotbank (38) and Housesteads (37). Smaller blocks were used for the quoins (the corner stones) and voussoirs. The fact that similar features were observed at Milecastle 40 (Winshields) further indicates that the milecastles were constructed in pairs. The smaller block size may be explained by the difficulty of bringing the sandstone across the wet ground from the south, although this does not seem to have deterred the builders of Milecastle 41 (Shield-on-the-Wall), one of the most remote on the entire line.

FIGURE 17 A chamfered stone found in Peel Gap. In its original setting the chamfer faces downwards and the white line marks the junction with the curtain wall. The traces of whitewash on this stone are important evidence that parts of Hadrian's Wall were painted white in antiquity.
(Photo: J. Crow, 1986)

At Castle Nick recent excavations have showed that there were early timber buildings in the interior belonging to the construction period of both the milecastle and the adjacent wall. With its sheltered position and good access through the Whin Sill, the milecastle at Castle Nick served as a small base for the construction works on the Wall. Immediately afterwards a barrack block was constructed on the east side, with timber structures west of the central roadway. The first barrack did not last long, probably because the ground was wetter on the east side, and it was replaced by a stone-built barrack on the west, which butted up against the inner, west wall of the milecastle. The north gate was surmounted by a tower similar in size to a turret. The remains of stone window heads with a chevron design were found close to the tower.

At Milecastle 37 (Housesteads) the north gateway is the best extant example of a milecastle gate, still surviving to the first arch stone or voussoir. The additional voussoirs now in position are a recent restoration, recovered from earlier excavations. Each block weighs up to 230 kg. In the upper face of each stone is a deeply angled slot, or lewis-hole, individually cut so that each stone was suspended from the hoist at the angle it was to occupy in the arch. The very size of the blocks used in the gate were to be the latter's undoing, for as the north arch slumped forward as a result of inadequate footings, the arch collapsed and sheared the long stones bonding the passage wall to the gate responds. In the past this collapse has been attributed to 'enemy action', during a supposed 'invasion' in AD 197. However, recent investigation shows that this catastrophe can be explained by an excess of monumentality and poor planning. It must have occurred soon after the gate was completed since the door stop was found to be unworn, in contrast to the one surviving in the south gate. After the collapse the north gate was blocked up with a clay-bonded wall to the same width as the Narrow Wall. This allowed passage along the wall-top across the site of the gate. It was probably felt adequate to leave access through the Wall to the north gate of the fort 400 m to the east. Part of the debris from the collapsed gate was reused in the later barrack and included a fragment of a building inscription originally set over the gate by men from the Second Augustan Legion, which is also known to have worked on milecastles 38 and 42. After this collapse it is unclear whether the milecastle was occupied at all in the later years of Hadrian's reign.

The Peel Gap tower

One of the final elements in the construction of Hadrian's Wall was the addition of an extra tower in Peel Gap. The discovery of this turret in 1986 came as a great surprise, since the only other additional tower to the sequence of turret–milecastle–turret was that at Pike Hill in Cumbria. The Peel Gap tower is identical in size to Turret 39a on the crag to the east, except that there is no recess into the south face of the Wall. The Peel Gap tower is clearly secondary, since its side walls butt against the existing Narrow Wall. Finds from inside and outside the tower show that it had a similar history and use to the neighbouring turrets. Within there was a sequence of hearths and a platform in the south-west corner, a feature found in many turrets and thought to have been the base for stairs. In the corners of the tower were two piles of small rounded pebbles, possibly the remains of sacks of crude slingshots. An unexpected discovery was the bolt-head from a ballista, a Roman small artillery piece. Evidence for such armaments has not been found before from turrets, although it is known from forts. Another potential missile from Peel Gap was a leather boot found in the peat to the north of the Wall. Perhaps it was lobbed at a scavenging dog by a bored and weary sentry.

FIGURE 18 View into Peel Gap from the east, with Hadrian's Wall in the foreground on the west end of Peel Crags. This position, or another to the west on the right side of the photograph, would have allowed much better points for observation along the Wall. (Photo: J. Crow 1986)

The Peel Gap tower raises two problems: first the discovery of an unexpected tower when both the predicted turrets are known, second, why should the extra tower be placed where it is? It has been recognised that the Wall-mile between Castle Nick and Winshields milecastles (39 and 40) is exceptionally long. In addition the distance between turrets 39a and 39b is particularly long, exceeding by 200 m the normal distance of 494 m between turrets. The tower at Peel Gap lies exactly mid-way between each turret: it would appear that regular spacing was the most important factor determining the location. Even so the tower's position often perplexes those who would prefer a tactical explanation for the siting of turrets and milecastles on the Wall.

The Peel Gap tower is located at the lowest point in the gap with very poor visibility to the north, west and east. These problems could easily have been remedied by placing the tower to overlook the gap either on the crags to the east or at the point where the Wall turns to the north on the west side of the gap. From both locations there is excellent all-round visibility as well as the possibility of observing neighbouring turrets (Figure 18). The Roman builders of the tower chose to ignore all these potential advantages. Instead, the location bisects the distance between the two existing turrets: spacing rather than tactical advantage determined the planning of the tower. The value of regular spacing can best be understood in terms of the need for access to the Wall and its patrol-walk. The Roman army is sometimes criticised for excessive rigidity and dogmatism, yet at Housesteads during the construction of the fort, the north-east angle tower was moved so as to occupy a position in relation to Hadrian's Wall that allowed better access between the tower and the wall-walk. The discovery of an additional turret at Peel Gap suggests that Roman commanders perceived the role of turrets on Hadrian's Wall as places for patrolling and secure access up to the Wall, not necessarily as observation points over long distances. To carry out surveillance effectively it was necessary to pound along the wall-top, not just sit in the comfort of the turrets and milecastles. The finds from these structures have all the appearance of mess rooms, with gaming boards and pottery mugs, possibly used for drinking weak beer.

The Vallum

The Vallum is known to have been constructed after many of the forts were built and it is possible that work began on this structure before building resumed on the Wall itself. The Vallum comprised a wide, steep-sided ditch, with parallel mounds to the north and south of it. More nonsense has been written about it than any other element of the Wall system. It was not a canal, neither was it intended to have been defended as an outwork or as an earlier proto-Wall, as was once thought. It presented a formidable barrier to movement from north to south and could only be crossed at the forts (there are no known crossing-places elsewhere). Although it was possible to come through the Wall at the milecastle gateways, the audacious traveller also needed to cross the Vallum mounds and ditch, which must have presented a considerable obstacle. Normally the Vallum runs close to the Wall but from Sewingshields westwards it follows the base of the Whin Sill's tail so that it could be excavated in soil rather than through rock or across boggy land. In this the Roman builders seem to have learnt from their earlier experience at Limestone Corner to the east of Carrawburgh, where the Vallum ditch was cut from solid whinstone, a remarkable, if rather bullheaded, achievement. It is significant that so much effort was expended on the Vallum ditch at this place, since the Wall-ditch (ie the V-shaped ditch running parallel to the north of Hadrian's Wall) was abandoned, a measure of the significance which the Romans held this element in the Wall system.

A new frontier

The history of Hadrian's Wall and its forts during the Antonine period (AD 138–93) remains obscure. The majority of the auxiliary garrisons on the northern British frontier were now stationed in Scotland, on the Antonine Wall begun in AD 146 by Hadrian's successor, Antoninus Pius. Some garrisons may well have continued at Housesteads and on the Wall itself, as there is no clear indication of any break in occupation of the turrets and milecastles in the 'Housesteads Command'. The pottery, still the principal dating evidence, cannot by itself be dated sufficiently closely to show any clear hiatus, so that we cannot be certain if there was any attempt to demilitarise the mural barrier on Hadrian's Wall, as has been suggested in the past.

There is better evidence for the recommissioning of the Wall in the later second century following the abandonment of the Antonine Frontier after AD 162. This is best seen at Sycamore Gap, where a length of early-type wall with a regular levelling course can be seen on the north face. Excavation showed that this section of the Wall was repaired with lime mortar and the construction deposits sealed pottery datable to the later second century, suggesting post-Antonine repairs at this point. Included among the debris left by the work gangs was a stone-cut gaming board, too heavy to take away, and a decorated window arch-stone, similar to those from Housesteads, that was reused in the Wall repairs. These are the only repairs on the Wall that can be dated archaeologically by artefacts, and immediately to the east of them the character of the Wall changes radically. The line of the thin levelling course is broken and the core and face are bonded with a hard white mortar. This is clearly later than the post-Antonine repair in the bottom of the gap and represents evidence for the massive reconstruction of Hadrian's Wall undertaken in the early third century under the Severan emperors.

Native settlement

At some point between the re-establishment of the Wall as a frontier in the 160s and the Severan restorations of the early third century the Vallum went out of use. It has long been presumed that the Vallum's purpose was to exclude the native civilian population from the military zone, but a reassessment of the evidence from the native settlement at Milking Gap indicates that the latter may not have been abandoned throughout the period the Vallum was in service. The settlement at Milking Gap, situated between the Wall and the Vallum, represents a typical Romano-British farmstead common in the uplands of northern England. It consists of a sub-rectangular enclosure containing a circular stone structure with internal dividing walls radiating out from it, possibly stock yards for cattle (Figure 19). Two smaller huts stand each side of the entrance in the south-east angle and two further huts butt up against the south wall. It has been suggested that occupation was forcibly ended by the Roman army at the time of the building of the Vallum (Breeze and Dobson 1976, 206). However, there is no actual evidence (such as layers of burning or visible destruction) for this and the hypothesis relates to the presumption that the Vallum was built to exclude civilian occupation. The presence of a smaller building added to the enclosure implies a longer period of development of the settlement before and during the occupation of the Wall. More evidence for Romano-British settlement is represented by an area of cord rig in the south-east corner of the Roman temporary camp known as Haltwhistle Burn 2 at Cawfields.

It is possible that the settlement above Bradley Farm discovered in 1988 may also

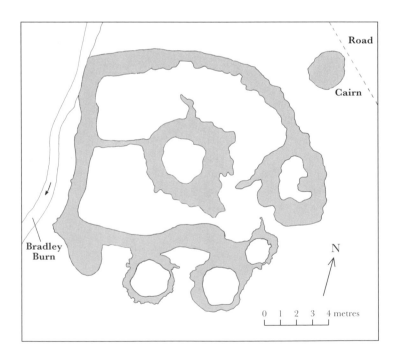

FIGURE 19
Milking Gap
native settlement.
(After Kilbride-
Jones, 1934)

be Romano-British in date. It consists of four hut circles measuring between 4.7 and 5.3 m internally, with walls up to 0.4 m high, enclosed by a boulder wall, within which are traces of two internal divisions. The site, situated high on the southern slope of the Whin Sill, is characteristic of settlement of this period. It has not yet been excavated, but could possibly be contemporary with the late Romano-British settlement at nearby Milking Gap. No further investigation has yet been made of the so-called Romano-British settlement just outside the Trust estate on Winshields discovered by H. MacLauchlan during his survey of the Wall in the 1850s (MacLauchlan 1857). What effect the arrival of the Romans had on the native population remains uncertain. One settlement lying just outside the estate in Crindledykes Farm could provide some information. It consists of a number of earthwork enclosures and field walls and is cut by a quarry which may be Roman. It is partly overlaid by two, if not three, sub-rectangular enclosures, one of which contains the outline of a round house, common to many Romano-British settlements. Furthermore, detailed examination of recent aerial photographs taken by Tim Gates in 1992 has revealed yet more evidence of native settlement to the north of the Wall, in particular one lying just to the west of the Black Dyke within the National Trust estate. The relationship between these settlements and the Roman Wall is as yet not known.

The vicus

Wherever the Roman army set up a permanent station, a civilian settlement, known as a *vicus*, soon sprang up outside its walls. *Vici* are known from every fort along the line of the Wall and the example at Housesteads is probably one of the best preserved. The *vicus* is concentrated around the south, east and west gates of the fort and along the line of the roads leading south to the Stanegate at Vindolanda and Grindon. Twenty-six buildings have been excavated or traced, although only six are on display, the best-known part of the settlement located just outside the south gate of the fort. The original settlement may have been centred around the well on the bottom of the slope by Chapel Hill. Celtic associations with water deities, as known from Coventina's Well at Carrawburgh, could have led to this area becoming the religious focus for the settlement, and later the location of the temple of Mithras, or *mithraeum*, and the shrine to the god Mars Thincus. The other focus of settlement lies just outside the fort. The stone-built *vicus* outside the south gate has been traditionally dated to the late second century, after the Vallum had been decommissioned, but excavations have revealed earlier timber buildings beneath the surviving structures, although these have not been dated. It is possible that the *vicus* was rebuilt in stone about the time when terraces were built into the hillside in *c.*AD 200 (Crow 1995).

Most of the inhabitants of the *vicus* would have been civilians, camp followers and soldiers' servants. Traders and merchants supplying pottery, oil, fish sauce and olives from the western Mediterranean would also have found a ready-made market located outside the fort. A workshop producing metalwork has been identified by the presence of a small box furnace in Building IV and the entrance to Building II consists of two well-preserved slots, typical of Roman shops closed with shutters, as seen at Pompeii. One building may have been a tavern, no doubt an essential part of any *vicus*, with the owner's quarters at the rear and above. Many of the buildings in the settlement were for domestic use and the long narrow houses, otherwise known as strip houses, found at Housesteads, with their short axis aligned on to the street, are typical of *vicus* buildings found in Britain and Germany. Other houses can be identified by the presence of domestic shrines, one of which depicts the Genii Cucullati (a triad of local Romanised gods) set in a carefully built stone apse, and the tavern contained a *genius* or guardian spirit. Not all houses were so well built and the rough-and-ready construction of a series of buildings south of Building VII revealed evidence of occupation by Germanic troops, the Cuneus Frisiorum, who formed part of the third-century garrison of the fort (Crow 1995). Incidentally, the museum built by the National Trust in 1936 at Housesteads is a reconstruction of one of the *vicus* buildings.

The Severan rebuilding of Hadrian's Wall

A fourth-century biography of Septimius Severus, who became emperor in AD 193, records that he built the Wall in northern Britain and that it was 'the greatest glory of his reign'. Over the centuries antiquaries and archaeologists have argued about whether the builder of the Roman Wall in Northumberland and Cumbria was in fact Hadrian or Severus. It is now clear from the surviving structural evidence that both emperors were responsible for massive building and rebuilding of the Wall.

The reconstruction of the first Narrow Wall took a number of forms: in places on Highshield Crags the earlier walls were completely erased and the hard white mortar of the rebuild clings tenaciously to the whinstone bedrock (Figure 20). The extent of the reconstruction obviously varied according to the survival and state of the Hadrianic Wall. In other places on Highshield Crags the rebuilders sealed up to two courses of the earlier unmortared Wall by later construction (Figure 21). In Peel Gap the new wall was constructed on the demolished stump of Hadrian's Wall and was considerably narrower (by 450 mm) than the earlier Narrow Wall. This sequence of narrow and extra-narrow walls can be seen in many places in the middle lengths of the Wall from Sewingshields to Cawfields, and has also been recorded east of the North Tyne river on Stagshaw Common and Planetrees, where the Wall was only saved from destruction in 1801 by the special pleading of William Hutton (Hutton 1802).

The quality of the reconstruction work, in particular the hardness and durability of the lime mortar, ensures that most of the visible lengths in the middle sections belong to the Severan rebuild. This fact has not always been recognised and the

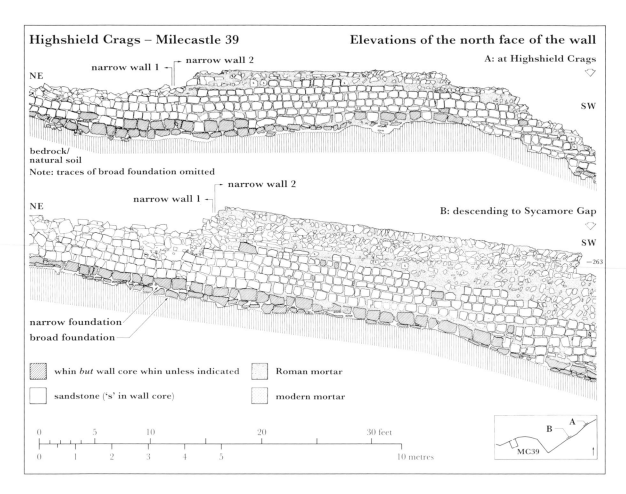

Highshield Crags – Milecastle 39

Elevations of the north face of the wall

A: at Highshield Crags

NE

narrow wall 1

narrow wall 2

SW

bedrock/
natural soil

Note: traces of broad foundation omitted

narrow wall 1

narrow wall 2

NE

B: descending to Sycamore Gap

SW

—263

narrow foundation

broad foundation

whin *but* wall core whin unless indicated

Roman mortar

sandstone ('s' in wall core)

modern mortar

| 0 | | 5 | | 10 | | | 20 | | | 30 feet |
| 0 | 1 | 2 | 3 | 4 | 5 | | | | 10 metres | |

B A

MC39

FIGURE 20 Elevation drawings of Hadrian's Wall on Highshield Crags. As part of the excavation programme the Wall was fully recorded in plan and elevation. The lower drawing shows the highest surviving length of Hadrian's Wall. (B. Williams)

FIGURE 21 Hadrian's Wall on Highshield Crags with Winshields in the distance. To the left is the reconstructed later, narrow wall with the earlier Hadrianic Narrow Wall in the foreground. (Photo: J. Crow, 1984)

editors of *The Roman Inscriptions in Britain* mistakenly observed of a fragment of a Roman tombstone on Peel Crags that it 'has been reused in some modern rebuilding of the Wall' (Collingwood and Wright 1965, 521, 1641). It is in fact set in good Roman mortar typical of the later reconstruction. John Clayton, the nineteenth-century antiquary, was in a better position to distinguish ancient work from recent restoration and he observed of the Wall on Highshield Crags that it 'was so very genuine, that I do not like to renew these little fallings away' (Clayton 1855a, 56). Recent excavations have shown that this wall stands in places to a height of over 3 m, the tallest original piece of Roman masonry surviving from the Wall. Detailed analysis of the mortar has shown that the Roman builders were very careful to select a particular type of limestone for making their mortars. Limestone and sandstone outcrop frequently in the neighbourhood of the Wall, and there are over twenty separate limestone seams parallel to the Whin Sill and up to 2 km to the north and south of it. It is clear that only specific limestones were used by the later builders of the Severan wall, the result of over a century's trial and testing of the resources of the district. The results of this empirically gained knowledge stand as a monument to Roman mortar technology, as impressive in the harsh landscape of Northumberland as the great imperial baths and basilicas of Rome itself.

The reconstruction of the Wall at this time can also be recognised in the vertical offsets, as they are called, in the south face of the Wall. These can be seen in a number of places, particularly in the section of Wall from Housesteads to Hotbank that was partly restored by John Clayton. In the past some archaeologists thought that these features belonged to the Victorian work, but it is now quite certain that the changes are part of the rebuilding of the Wall. The offsets mark lengths of the curtain, ranging in length from 6.7 m to 20.1 m, which have been taken down and later rebuilt. A common experience encountered in the rebuilding of field walls and other structures today is that once the wall has been demolished, there are never sufficient corestones or filling to reinstate it to exactly its original dimensions, so new stones are invariably required. This seems also to have been the experience of the Roman builders, who chose instead to construct an extra-narrow wall, using the harder mortars that had become available, rather than lead in new corestone.

At the same time as the Wall itself was being rebuilt the milecastles and turrets underwent major alterations and changes. The turret at Peel Gap was modified later in the second century. Several hearths have been found within the tower, but at a late date the interior was closed off when the ground-floor door was blocked. This has happened in other turrets including the neighbouring tower at Steel Rigg (39b). Even when the lower part of the turret was abandoned the upper part continued to function in some way. At Peel Gap, before the tower was completely demolished, a platform was constructed on the west side (see Figure 18). This feature has no parallel in other turrets, and was probably the base for a ladder leading on to the wall-top and the upper part of the tower.

Whilst the Wall was undergoing restoration, the turrets between the milecastles were demolished, leaving a walkway across the earlier recesses. At Peel Crags turret (39a) the recess was filled up with long stone blocks, which can be recognised in the south face of the Wall (see Figure 15). Before this the interior of the turret appears to have fallen out of use and, uniquely, was used for burials (Simpson, G. 1976, 100; Crow and Jackson 1997, 65). The origin of the stone blocks reused in the recess is not known. It is not clear whether, once all the turrets in this sector had been demolished, there was still a need for continued access on to the top of the Wall. If so, access could have been provided by wooden ladders but these would have left little or no trace. The filling-in of the turret recesses suggests, however, that there remained a need to provide a wall-walk for the rebuilt Wall. Certainly there is plenty of evidence for the use of chamfered string-course blocks in the rebuilding of the Wall.

At Milecastle 39 (Castle Nick) the interior buildings underwent a variety of changes, which cannot be precisely dated. The barrack on the west side was modified and a row of smaller buildings was added on the east side of the road. Some of these had internal hearths and so were probably used for cooking and other domestic activities. One notable feature was the way that some of the east buildings had porches or verandas built on to the central roadway. In discussions of milecastles it is often assumed that the roadway through the milecastle was of continuing importance. At Castle Nick this passage was restricted from the late second century to pedestrian traffic and pack animals only. Stretches of road surfaces have survived inside the milecastle but cannot be traced outside, either to the south or to the north. The central roadway was in effect a central yard, not a thoroughfare. Both the gates at Castle Nick were narrowed, probably in the third century, again reflecting these changes inside the milecastle, and this phenomenon has been seen in other milecastles including Winshields (40). At the same time that access was being reduced in many milecastles, the north entrance at Housesteads (37) was opened up at a higher level above the earlier blocking, but as a narrow postern gate. No independent dating evidence survives, but this could be associated with the rebuilding of the Wall and the need for access on to the north side during the building operations. A building inscription of the Sixth Legion from York was found at the foot of the crags and could be associated with this rebuilding work.

Although the third-century rebuilding of Hadrian's Wall is best known from historical rather than epigraphic sources, one group of inscriptions may belong to this phase of work on Hadrian's Wall. These relate not to the centuries of Roman soldiers either building or restoring the Wall, but to levies from the tribes in the south-west of Britain, the Dumnonii from Devon and the Durotriges from Dorset. Two inscriptions of the Durotriges have been found between Housesteads and Great Chesters, and one of the Dumnonii to the west of Carvoran. Given the scale of the Severan reconstruction it is likely that both tribes participated in the rebuilding, especially as many of the local garrisons were likely to have been engaged in

FIGURE 22 Late 'chalet'-type barrack in the south-west corner of Milecastle 39 (Castle Nick), with central roadway in the foreground. (Photo: J. Crow, 1985)

the restoration work at the forts which is reported at this time in many inscriptions from Housesteads and elsewhere.

After the early third-century reconstruction little is known of the later history of the Wall. Excavations at Sycamore Gap revealed a hoard of coins datable to AD 350–60 buried in soil at the base of the Wall. These were later covered by rubble and debris when the Wall decayed, but at the time of their burial the Wall still stood to full height. Only in later times was it to become a local quarry and source for stone. Whereas almost all the turrets were demolished in the third century, most milecastles continued to be occupied into the following century. At Castle Nick the barrack on the west of the central road was first reduced in length, and then replaced by a row of two or three small structures, similar in plan to the so-called 'chalets' found in the fourth-century fort (see below), although much smaller in size (Figure 22). A number of structural alterations followed, including the addition of curved porches constructed on to the road surface. Similar additional features were noted in the chalets overlying Barrack XIII at Housesteads, suggesting that close contact remained between the fort and milecastle. Towards the end of the fourth century, part of the east side of the interior of Castle Nick was used as a dump, but occupation continued in the buildings on the west side. Nothing is known of the immediate post-Roman occupation, but the area around Castle Nick had become a shieling ground by the fourteenth century at the latest.

The end of Roman occupation

The late third and fourth centuries AD saw changes to the Roman army that would affect the arrangements in the forts and along the line of the Wall. The barrack blocks at Housesteads were totally replanned and rebuilt to form a line of separate structures, normally detached from their neighbours, often referred to as 'chalets'. In the third century, soldiers were allowed to marry and it has been suggested that the barrack blocks were converted from military to civilian use, to house the soldiers and their families, and thus cutting down the size of the garrison (Daniels 1989). This, however, seems unlikely – it is all too easy to impose twentieth-century ideas of provision and welfare on to the Roman period. The billeting of troops in the *vicus*, however, could go some way to explain the reduction of the number of barracks in the fort. The milecastles were still occupied well into the fourth century but it has not been possible to determine the make-up of their garrisons. They may have been homes for a small number of men and their families, farming the nearby land whilst still being paid by a central authority, and carrying out military duty only when required (Johnson 1989, 111). Despite the fact that the latest building inscription known from Hadrian's Wall dates to between AD 296 and AD 305, there is evidence for rebuilding and rearrangement of the interior of the forts and the Wall during the fourth century, and it is known that the defences at Housesteads were improved in the fourth century (Crow 1995). The garrisons on the Wall still saw action at this time, however, most notably against the Picts in the early fourth century and the so-called 'Barbarian Conspiracy' of Picts, Dicalydones, Verturiones and others who attacked not only the north but also the southern shores of the province in AD 367–8. However, there is little archaeological evidence for any hostile raids or destruction on the northern frontier in the fourth century. The continued maintenance of Storehouse XV at Housesteads throughout the fourth century reveals that a system of provision for the Wall garrisons was maintained and evidence from Milecastle 39 testifies to continuing occupation through this period.

The evidence for the end of Roman occupation of Housesteads and the Wall comes from the breakdown of the supply of coins, metalwork and pottery at the end of the fourth century (Crow 1995). Although Britain remained strategically important to the Empire, troops were often withdrawn from the province to help bolster rival claims to the imperial throne. By AD 410 (the traditionally accepted date for the end of Roman rule), realising that no more pay would be forthcoming, the garrisons abandoned military installations. In contrast to many other forts along the line of the Wall, Housesteads presents no evidence for definite post-Roman occupation. It would seem that after almost 300 years of occupation, Hadrian's Wall, certainly in the middle lengths, no longer served its role as a boundary between Roman and Barbarian and gradually fell into disuse and disrepair.

4

THE FOREST OF LOWES

Britain has kings, but they are tyrants; she has judges, but they are wicked ... bloody, proud and murderous, adulterers and enemies of God.

(Gildas 1978, 27.1)

The exact date when Roman occupation of Housesteads and the milecastles along the Wall ended is not known. Housesteads is almost alone amongst the Wall forts in not revealing any certain evidence for post-Roman occupation. The post-Roman period in Britain is often difficult to chart not only because of the scarcity of adequate archaeological and documentary evidence but also because of the number of legends and pseudo-histories, mostly associated with King Arthur, from which even Hadrian's Wall is not immune. The archaeological evidence that does survive is often very faint, identifiable only through detailed and painstaking excavation, and, ironically, much late- and post-Roman material is likely to have been destroyed by antiquarian excavators eager to dig down to the earlier and more abundant layers. What is certain, however, is that the end of Roman Britain was not brought about by an orgy of violent destruction, as depicted in popular accounts, and that the breakdown of Roman institutions and the development of sub-Roman and early medieval societies was far more complex than has previously been thought.

British settlement

Palaeobotanical evidence from Crag Lough and elsewhere suggests a period of relative stability after the end of the Roman period. Cereal pollen (large *Gramineae*) is still abundant in the early fifth century, as is hazel, which was coppiced for its wood and nuts. It is only much later that reafforestation occurs and the open heathland is once again replaced by mixed deciduous woodland, although this process may have begun in the fourth century. Dates for the regeneration of woodland range from AD 460 ± 60 at Steng Moss and AD 620 ± 40 at Fell End, associated with a decline in cereal pollen and other anthropogenic indicator plants, after which the region entered a period of 'agricultural dormancy' (Dark and Dark, 1996). What is surprising is that this change was localised to the northern military zone and nowhere else in the former province of Britain was there any significant reafforestation. It can be argued that the Roman army made intensive and specific demands on the landscape; once the garrisons were removed, less intensive land use continued until the seventeenth and eighteenth centuries.

It is possible that the population of Housesteads, which would have been fairly small at the end of the Roman period, moved down to the more sheltered settlement at Vindolanda. An early Christian gravestone (one of very few in the north of England) bearing the name Brigomaglos was discovered here, as well as some Anglo-Saxon remains, indicating that Vindolanda continued to be occupied in the post-Roman period. The hill-fort on Barcombe Hill, overlooking Vindolanda, was reoccupied during the early medieval period, possibly by the descendants of the garrison, and may have retained elements of the original name of Housesteads, Vercovicium. The fort at Great Chesters may also hold evidence for post-Roman activity. Its Roman name, Aesica, appears to have survived into the seventh

FIGURE 23 St Cuthbert, Northumbria's most famous saint, refusing a bishopric from King Egfrid and Bishop Trumwine, AD 734. (National Trust Photographic Library)

century, when a life of St Cuthbert recounts a miracle at Ahse (Figure 23). The saint was travelling from Hexham towards Carlisle along either the Stanegate or the Military Way (routes that remained important until the building of the Military Road by General Wade in the 1750s), when he stopped at a *mansio*, or building, about mid-way. People 'gathered around from the mountains' to Ahse to see the saint, who blessed and preached to them and miraculously cured a boy. Ahse is described as a district, not a place, and if the identification with Aesica is accepted, it demonstrates how Roman names could persist even when the settlements them-selves had withered away (Crow 1995). Incidentally, Cuddy's Crags and Cutty Well House, the original name for the farm cottage north of the Winshield Crags, may also be associated with the much-travelled saint (Watson 1970, 80).

The Roman forts retained an importance amongst the local population long after they had ceased to function. Some developed into religious centres, such as Bewcastle in Cumbria, where in the seventh century a large, carved stone cross was erected. Housesteads, too, may have retained such a significance, although it failed to develop to the same scale as Bewcastle. A small chapel-like structure 6 m wide and at least 10 m long has been identified in the north part of the fort. Not far from the apsidal building a Roman watertank was reused as a cist burial, or stone-lined grave, a feature commonly associated with the early Christian period in northern Britain. The proximity of the apsidal structure to the east–west-orientated long cist suggests that the former may have been a church, perhaps originally serving the late fourth-century garrison at Housesteads, but the presence of a burial within the fort walls suggests that the site retained its religious significance after it had ceased to be occupied (Crow 1995).

A long-forgotten reign

The fifth and sixth centuries saw the emergence of small tribal kingdoms on both sides of the Roman Wall. In the north, the tribe once known as the Votadini (whose lands covered parts of southern Scotland and northern England) re-emerged as the Goddodin, whose activities were recorded in the eponymous poem. In the west Rheged rose to become an important British kingdom. The economy was based largely on subsistence farming and livestock, but raiding and slave-trading seem also to have been important activities. These sub-Roman kingdoms retained a few memories of the imperial past – kings assumed Latin names such as Tacitus and Coroticus and Christian tombstones were engraved with the legend *hic iacit*, 'here lies'.

By the sixth century, an accurate memory of the great linear boundary in the north of its former island province seems to have been lost to the surviving Roman Empire on the Mediterranean fringe. The historian Procopius, writing in Constantinople at this time, knew of the Wall only through legends and stories:

Moreover, in this isle of Brittia, men of ancient time built a long wall, cutting off a great portion of it: for the soil, and the man, and all other things, are not alike on both sides; for on the eastern [southern] side of the Wall, there is a wholesomeness of air in conformitywith the seasons, moderately warm in summer, and cool in winter. Many men inhabit here, living much as other men. The trees, with their appropriate fruits, flourish in season, and their corn lands are as productive as others; and the district appears sufficiently fertilized by streams. But on the western [northern] side all is different, insomuch, indeed, that it would be impossible for a man to live there, even for half an hour. Vipers and serpents innumerable, with all other kinds of wild beasts, infest that place; and, what is most strange, the natives affirm, that if any one, passing the Wall, should proceed to the other side, he would die immediately, unable to endure the unwholesomeness of the atmosphere. Death also, attacking such beasts as go thither, forthwith, destroys them. ... They say that the souls of men departed are always conducted to this place. (Book 8, *Wars*, xx, 42–6).

Contemporary native historians were also vague about the origin and purpose of the great Wall. Gildas, the sixth-century cleric, recounts the story of the building of the Wall in his work *de Excidio Britanniae et Conquestu* (*The Ruin of Britain*). He erroneously states that the great wall was built *after* the departure of the Romans, first by the 'leaderless and irrational' British in turf (presumbly he means the Vallum) and later, after more incursions by the Picts, the Romans returned to build another wall in stone, 'quite different from the first. This one ran from sea to sea, linking towns that happened to have been sited there out of fear of the enemy' (Gildas 1978, 18.2). Even Bede, the seventh-century monk writing from Jarrow on the opposite bank of the Tyne to Wallsend, was not able to understand fully the correct historical context of the Wall, and echoed Gildas in his placing of the construction of two separate walls well into the fifth century, long after the Romans had departed. He was able to provide a description, however, stating it to be 2.4 m wide and 3.6 m high. Bede's figures are not corroborated by later observers, who described the Wall as being higher than he recorded it. Bede, of course, was writing about only one length of Wall, and different sections may have survived to a greater or lesser extent than the section he observed. Furthermore, it is not impossible that different lengths of the Wall may actually have been built at different heights, although no evidence survives to prove this theory.

The Anglo-Saxon kingdom of Northumbria began as two separate kingdoms, Deira and Bernicia, based around North Yorkshire and modern Northumberland respectively. What influence the arrival of the Anglo-Saxons had on the remaining communities around the middle lengths of the Wall is unknown and the archaeological data is limited. Claims that Housesteads was held and re-defended in the Dark Ages are based on the incorrect identification of a spearhead as Anglo-Saxon (Dark 1992, 111). It is in fact a type well attested amongst Roman finds (Crow 1995). The nearest Anglo-Saxon material discovered in the area comes from Vindolanda, where an annular brooch and a possibly fifth- or sixth-century penannular brooch were recently discovered, and there is evidence for the re-defence of the curtain walls, although this does not necessarily indicate Anglo-Saxon occupation. The legend that the Black Dyke was the frontier between the British and Anglo-Saxon kingdoms is intriguing, as there is plenty of evidence to show that the Anglo-Saxons often buried their dead along the line of prehistoric and Roman boundaries, as well as in earlier burial mounds, henges and hill-forts, to demarcate territory and to protect the rights of inheritance of the kin (Higham 1993, 70). No such burials are known from the line of the Black Dyke, but it is known that in the Middle Ages it formed part of the boundary of the Barony of Wark (Spain 1921, 121). The only possible Anglo-Saxon settlement in South Tynedale may have been at Beltingham, whose name may derive from the Anglo-Saxon for *ing* meaning 'people', *ham* meaning 'village' and *belt*, probably a corruption of a leader's name. The remains of an Anglo-Saxon cross-base are known from Beltingham, however. It was later the site of a medieval chapel and a religious focus for the South Tyne valley.

The founding of the kingdom of Northumbria in the seventh century changed the political orientation from north–south to east–west. No longer did Hadrian's Wall form the line, frontier or otherwise, between two political or military entities. The kingdom of Northumbria, with its centre originally at Bamburgh and later at Yeavering, stretched northwards well into southern Scotland. The line of the Wall, therefore, was disregarded, which suggests that by this time it was both structurally and functionally obsolete. Sub-Roman reoccupation of the Wall by a native population, as suggested by Dark and Dark (1996), might account for the absence of Anglo-Saxon finds in the area, but would have been short-lived. The rapid collapse of the British kingdoms in the early seventh century was probably due as much to political as to military reasons.

The Liberty of Tynedale

At its height in the seventh and eighth centuries, the Kingdom of Northumbria covered an area largely contemporary with modern-day Northumberland, Tyne and Wear, Durham and North Yorkshire and extended into southern Scotland. However, there is no archaeological or documentary evidence for habitation on the upper reaches of the Tyne valley and it is not until the twelfth century that there is any evidence of settlement returning to the vicinity of the Wall. The Norman invasions of the eleventh century desolated the north but had also established a new aristocracy in the region. The name of the nearby town of Haltwhistle derives from the Norman French 'haute', meaning 'high', and the Saxon 'twisle', meaning 'the meeting of two rivers', in this case the Haltwhistle Burn and the South Tyne (Watson 1970). In 1157 Henry I awarded the Liberty of Tynedale, ie most of south-west Northumberland, to the Scottish king, Malcolm, who in 1165 passed it on to his brother, William the Lion. It was to remain in Scottish hands until Edward I won it back for England in 1289 (Moore 1915). In 1296 Northumberland was raided by an incursion of Scottish highlanders, who sacked Hexham Abbey, murdering the canons or forcing them to disperse. The following year the Scots returned under the leadership of William Wallace, who took the last of the Abbey's silver before returning to Scotland. The population of the uplands, greatly disturbed by the Scottish invasions, slowly returned to its previous numbers, but the value of the land was reduced by almost two-thirds.

Within the Liberty lay the Huntlands of Tindale, the ancient name of the wastes and moors lying between the Wall and the North Tyne. The area is also known as the Forest of Lowes, although the two are not necessarily synonymous as the latter refers more to the area surrounding the Wall containing Broomlee, Crag, Greenlee and Grindon loughs, and a now-expired lough known as the Little Cow. Documents recall how David I of Scotland granted the land to Hextilda, countess of Ethehetala, a member of the Cumin family who owned it for six generations. The Huntlands, as the name suggests, were commonly used for hunting for the larder but were also prime shieling grounds (see below). Records recalling grants and leases for shielings date back to 1177 when William the Lion gave his esquire, Reginald Prat of Tynedale, 'four shielings wherever he pleased within the Huntland' (Hodgson 1840, 326).

Despite the fact that there are no documentary references to Housesteads during the medieval period, archaeological evidence for medieval settlement is known in the area of the estate. The so-called 'longhouse' (a single-storey dwelling divided

FIGURE 24 A possible peel tower on Steel Rigg, excavated by F. G. Simpson in 1911. (Museum of Antiquities, University of Newcastle upon Tyne)

into two parts, one for people the other for livestock) discovered by Bosanquet at Housesteads at the turn of the twentieth century may be medieval in date, but sadly it was greatly disturbed by later archaeologists digging down to the Roman deposits beneath. Further archaeological evidence of permanent settlement on the site is lacking, but the possibility of reoccupation during the climatic optimum of the thirteenth century, when England's climate was on average warmer and drier than in the following 500 years, cannot be ruled out. The reuse of the Roman terracing, noted in excavation (Frere 1987, 434; Daniels 1989, 55), suggests such a dry spell. Excavations along the line of Hadrian's Wall at Steel Rigg in 1911 revealed the location of a medieval building that may be a peel tower and which probably gave its name to Peel Gap and Peel Crags (Figure 24). Peel towers, or 'peles', are known throughout the Border lands between England and Scotland and provided defence and security for the occupants in this area troubled by warfare and banditry. Peels were built of stone, with walls of massive thickness, and ideally were three or four storeys high. The only entrance was through a double door at ground level, one of the doors being an outer iron gating, the other of oak reinforced with iron. The bottom storey was used as a store room and a spiral staircase led to the upper floors, which were used as living quarters. At the very top there was usually a beacon, to summon help in attack or to give warning of an impending foray (Fraser 1971, 52–3). The peel tower was usually a chiefly residence, but the unstrategic position of the peel at Steel Rigg suggests that it may have been only a farmhouse. Fragments of green-glazed vessels found during excavation have been dated to the fourteenth century (Simpson, G. 1976, 109).

North of Sewingshields Crags, just to the east of the estate boundary, on an old route leading from the South Tyne valley towards Wark and the North Tyne, are the remains of a medieval settlement. These consist of traces of a tower, fishponds and possibly a moated site, all characteristic of a manor of the thirteenth century, although it is thought that the earliest permanent settlement here dates back to the eleventh century (Crow 1995). Excavations at Milecastle 35 on Sewingshields Crags in the 1970s have shown something of the pattern of rural settlement in this area. The Roman milecastle had faded into total disuse before the site was reused in the thirteenth century, when the first of a number of longhouses was built. These provided accommodation for men and animals under the same roof. The remains of three longhouses, of varying plan when considered in detail, were identified at the site, which appears to have been abandoned in the early decades of the fifteenth century (Johnson 1989, 116). An interesting factor is the relative wealth of the finds from this settlement, which seem inappropriate for mere herdsmen. They include a decorated spur and a variety of glazed pottery, all more characteristic of a castle or a dwelling of high status. This suggests a possible use as a hunting lodge. An alternative explanation is that these treasures were robbers' loot hidden close to the notorious bandits' haunt at Busy Gap, less than a kilometre (half a mile) away (Crow 1995).

FIGURE 25 Aerial photograph of Bradley Green. The settlement is characterised by ridge and furrow and building platforms. The site of the gentleman's hall where Edward I stayed in 1306 may be underneath the nineteenth-century farmhouse. (T. Gates, 1992 © copyright reserved)

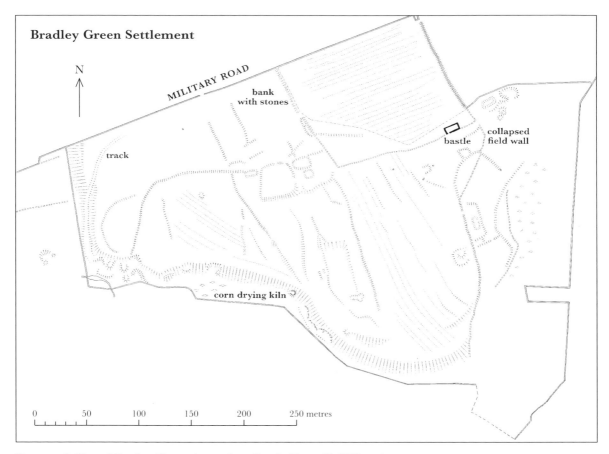

Bradley Green Settlement

N

MILITARY ROAD

bank
with stones

track

bastle   collapsed
          field wall

corn drying kiln

0   50   100   150   200   250 metres

FIGURE 26 Plan of Bradley Green deserted medieval village. (B. Williams)

Bradley Green

The most significant evidence of medieval settlement within the estate is at Bradley Green, a small triangle of land south of the Military Road opposite Bradley farmhouse (Figure 25). The triangle is formed on the east by the road leading down to Bardon Mill and on the west by the Bradley Burn. On the south side of the burn lies Bradley Hall, which is known to date back to at least the early fourteenth century if not before. Within the boundaries of Bradley Green lie the remains of medieval fields and traces of a settlement that never quite succeeded as a village, located on the marginal land between the uplands and the valley.

A Border Survey of 1541 notes that this part of the Wall country had once 'diverse townships and hamlets that were in times past inhabited, now lying desolate and waste' (Hodgson 1840, 326). The remains at Bradley Green consist of grass-covered depressions which were houses of various sizes, mostly aligned with a large bank apparently dividing the cultivated land to the south from the waste to the north. The field systems contain characteristically medieval 'inverted-S'-shaped ridge and furrow cultivation on the south-facing slope leading to the ledge above the burn, and a series of strip fields, or cultivation terraces, can also be identified. Later remains are also known from this site, including a pair of late sixteenth- to early seventeenth-century bastle houses (fortified houses) and a corn-drying kiln (a hollow in a bank for drying corn). The field is divided east and west by a collapsed dry-stone wall (Figure 26).

The settlement at Bradley Green is almost certainly associated with Bradley Hall, and was perhaps where the owner's bondsmen lived in the fourteenth century. The present-day farm of Bradley Hall dates to the nineteenth century, with foundations rebuilt from a sixteenth-century bastle house, but in the fourteenth century a building bearing that name was important enough to offer accommodation for a king. In 1306 Edward I and his retinue rested here on the 5th and 6th September as he progressed across England to Carlisle along the Stanegate (known as Karelgate (Carlisle Street) in the Middle Ages) (Hodgson 1840, 326). From Tynedale Edward passed to Lanercost Priory, where he spent the winter before assembling his army at Burgh-by-Sands for an invasion of Scotland that was to be curtailed by his death. It is inconceivable that a proud and terminally ill king and his entourage would rest in anything less than a large and well-guarded tower or tower house. No evidence of one survives however, although it may well have been on the site of the later bastle house.

With the exception of Edward I's visit in 1306 there is little documentary evidence referring to Bradley Hall or Bradley Green. It is known, however, that a family took its name from the place. Richard de Bradley, son of Henry, married Matilda, daughter of Nicholas de Thorngrafton and received land in Thorngrafton as part of the marriage agreement (Hodgson 1840, 326). The date of the wedding is unknown but it must have occurred in the thirteenth century as the settlement was made a century after an ancestor of Nicholas de Thorngrafton donated land to Hexham Priory in the twelfth century. It is possible that the de Bradley family built a tower house and called it Bradley Hall. Surprisingly, the itinerary of Edward's march across England does not mention the owners of Bradley and nor do the de Bradley family chronicles mention the king's visit. Perhaps by then Richard de Bradley had moved to his new possession in Thorngrafton. Certainly by 1326 Bradley Hall had passed into the hands of Adam de Swyneburne of Thirlwall who, on his death in that year, left it to his eldest daughter, Barnaba. However, Bradley Hall's importance must have been short-lived as it does not appear in the 1415 list of Border strongholds.

Settlement at Bradley Hall seems to date from a warm period known as the 'Little Optimum', which lasted from 700 to 1300, and was followed by the cooler 'Little Ice Age' that continued until 1850. One consequence of this warm period was the increase in population throughout Britain in the twelfth and thirteenth centuries, creating greater pressure for arable land, and a corresponding expansion of settlement into marginal upland areas, such as at Bradley Green, Sewingshields and possibly Housesteads. After the expansion into the uplands, the fourteenth century brought a series of crises. In 1312, Northumberland was once again invaded by the Scots, led by Robert the Bruce, who burned Hexham and Corbridge, and returned in 1314 to wreak further devastation on the countryside. A deterioration in climate between 1315 and 1318 resulted in catastrophic harvests throughout the country: the soils of the agriculturally marginal uplands, easily exhausted and vulnerable to climatic deterioration and crop failure, were especially badly affected. The pattern throughout the British Isles was one of an already weakened population which then succumbed to the Black Death in 1348 and beyond. Within two generations the population levels had fallen disastrously and by 1500 England was hardly more populous than at the time of the Domesday Book, almost 450 years earlier.

There is no mention of Bradley again until the sixteenth century, when a Border Survey of 1541 found it to be 'lying waste and unplenished'. Some years later, the Border Survey of 1552 ordered that 'two men about the town, Nicholas Malaper and Robert Lowes' of Thorngrafton 'keep watch the Beacons of Bradley', presumably Hotbank Crags (Hodgson 1840, 328). Bradley Hall, however, is marked on John Saxton's map of Northumberland dated c.1576. From the time of Edward I's wars against Scotland in the late thirteenth and early fourteenth centuries, the area surrounding Bradley lay in a region wracked by conflicts and banditry. The general lawlessness of the countryside led to the building of bastle houses; the remains of some can be seen incorporated into the later farmhouses at Bradley Hall and Grandy's Knowe, to the east of Bradley Green, as well as in Bradley Green itself. The Bradley Green bastle house has today been reduced to its foundations but nevertheless it is clear that its walls would have been massive. Large cornerstones are visible *in situ*, as are one or two doorstones. The bastle is slightly unusual in that the ground-floor entrance was in the centre of the south-facing long wall and not in a gable, but in other respects what is left conforms precisely to bastle specifications. Bastle houses are rarely found alone and the remains of another building can be seen just to the east.

Shielings and shieling grounds

> Here every way round about in the *wasts* as they term them, as also in Giliesland, you mey see as it were the ancient *Nomades*, a martiall kinde of men, who from the moneth of Aprill unto August, lye out scattering and summering (as they tearme it) with their cattell in little cottages here and there which they call *Sheales* and *Shealings*. (Camden 1722)

Camden, writing in 1599, was describing a form of pastoral activity known as 'transhumance', the seasonal migration of people and their herds from a winter settlement to a summer pasture. Today, the practice is still common in parts of Mediterranean Europe and Turkey, but in Britain it died out in the seventeenth century. The term 'shieling' refers to the hut or shelter occupied by the herdsmen and their families over the summer months and not to the pasture or the practice.

FIGURE 27 Shielings on Mons Fabricius, east of Milecastle 39 (Castle Nick). These structures date from the thirteenth to the sixteenth centuries and nestle behind the ruins of the Roman Wall. (Photo: J. Crow, 1984)

The summer pastures were known as shieling grounds and the custom was called 'summering' or 'shielding'. The word 'shieling' has been retained in many place-names, such as Highshield, Sewingshields and Shield-on-the-Wall, but its use is not restricted to pastoral areas and the term came to describe any small, seasonally occupied hut, such as the fishermen's huts at North Shields. The name is known to be Norse in origin and the practice of transhumance is thought to date back as far as the tenth century. Transhumance not only ensured the availability of animal fodder but also reduced the risk of disease which could wipe out valuable stock (Thirsk 1969, 22).

Many shielings were built of drystone walling with exterior walls up to 0.75 m thick. Most are rectangular in plan and vary in length from 4 m to 10 m by 2.2 m to 6 m wide. Many have interior partitions with walls much the same width as the exterior walls. Generally, there was only one entrance doorway, placed in or near the middle of the long wall. The only evidence for windows comes from a hut in the valley of the White Lyne, Cumbria, which had a small opening 0.3 m by 0.3 m wide and splayed internally to a width of 0.45 m. Most shielings may not have had a window at all. Roof-covering was almost certainly of turf (Ramm *et al.* 1970, 9–10). Shielings are often found in groups and the most detailed study yet carried out was in 1986, during the excavation of Hadrian's Wall on Mons Fabricius east of Castle Nick (Figure 27). A row of four shielings was built on the level hilltop, nestling into the collapse of the Wall; the rectangular houses with unmortared rubble-stone walls, measuring 8.5 m long by 2.5 m wide, had each been repaired and rebuilt a number of times. The earliest pottery dated to the fourteenth century, but later flagged floors and hearths could be dated to the early sixteenth century. A distinct trackway led up to the shielings around the side of the hill. Another scattered group of seven shielings was clustered around the lower slopes of the hill and over the ruins of Milecastle 39. Unlike the upper row, which had been constructed of stones from the Roman Wall, most of these used the unhewn whinstone boulders from the hillside. They were similar in area to the upper group but in part at least were constructed of turf. There were very few finds from the four that were excavated and it is difficult to say how many of these buildings were occupied simultaneously. Furthermore, it is not clear whether the upper group is contemporary with the lower group (Crow 1995).

One of the best-preserved groups of shielings on the estate is in the Bogle Hole, Shield-on-the-Wall Farm, where the shielings resemble a line of terraced houses sheltering in the gap. As previously mentioned, 'bogle' means 'ghost' in the local Northumberland dialect, and popular faith asserts that this was once the abode of evil spirits (Bruce 1851, 244). Many other shielings are known throughout the estate, for example, at Milking Gap, and east of the Knag Burn, to the north of Housesteads Fort. Another well-known group lies just outside the estate on

FIGURE 28 Reconstruction of shielings in Milecastle 35, c.1400, based on archaeological evidence excavated in the 1970s. (English Heritage)

(*Opposite*)
FIGURE 29 Distribution of shielings in the landscape as defined by township boundaries.

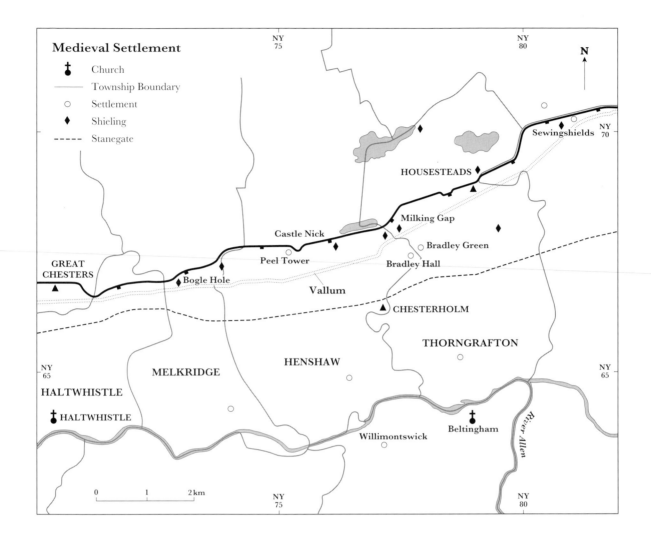

NY 75

NY 80

N

NY 70

NY 65

NY 65

NY 75

NY 80

Medieval Settlement

✝ Church

Township Boundary

○ Settlement

♦ Shieling

----- Stanegate

Sewingshields

HOUSESTEADS

Milking Gap

Castle Nick

Bradley Green

Peel Tower

Bradley Hall

GREAT
CHESTERS

♦ Bogle Hole

Vallum

CHESTERHOLM

THORNGRAFTON

HENSHAW

MELKRIDGE

HALTWHISTLE

✝ HALTWHISTLE

Willimontswick

Beltingham

River Allen

0   1   2km

Sewingshield Crags (Figure 28) and by Greenlee Lough, where fifteen shielings can be seen overlying the prehistoric enclosure (Ramm *et al.* 1970, 23).

The earliest records of shielings are usually to be found in the charters, leases and inquisitions of the twelfth, thirteenth and early fourteenth centuries. In 1177 King William the Lion of Scotland granted Reginald Prat of Tynedale a third of the manor of Haughton with four shielings to be established wherever he chose (Hodgson 1840, 2–3). In 1282 William de Swyneburne was granted a shieling at Greenlee and in 1326 Adam de Swyneburne held eight shielings in the Huntlands of Tynedale and another at Bradley 'in the manor of Henneshalgh [Henshaw]'. These documents reveal that the practice of transhumance was deeply embedded in the manorial structure of the Middle Ages and shieling grounds were the resource of the respective townships. The modern civil parishes closely resemble the township boundaries of the past and each cuts a long narrow transect across the full range of agricultural resources, from the meadow and arable of the Tyne valley, to the permanent and seasonal pasture of the upland and waste. Therefore, by using the First Edition Ordnance Survey Map of 1866 (sheet LXXXIII), it is possible to relate the known shielings to their appropriate townships, ie the group on Mons Fabricius were related to the township of Henshaw, and those at the Bogle Hole to that of Melkridge (Figure 29). Practices differed elsewhere and in Redesdale the allocation of the summer pastures was arranged by surname rather than by township, much like the clans of Scotland. The expedition was a social ceremony involving the whole community – no one was allowed to stay in the village nor stray from the main group 'in respect for ill neighbourhood and wronging one another' (Thirsk 1969, 22).

A second documentary source for shielings is the surveys and correspondence of the sixteenth and seventeenth centuries, although these are scarce and their scope is somewhat limited (Wrathmell 1975, 252). A survey of the Border lands carried out in 1603 recalls that the inhabitants of Tynedale 'for their shielding grownds they doe begyn and end by agrement among themselves according as the season falleth out' (Sanderson 1891, 52). What is known is that shielding was very lucrative for the landlords; in 1633 Lord William Howard, an influential landowner in both Northumberland and east Cumberland, received £25 5s in shieling rents and £95 15s 8d for the 'agistment', or feeding, of cattle (Thirsk 1975, 23). Large profits, however, inevitably drew the attention of the Border reivers and in 1597 the Warden of the English Middle Marches wrote complaining that he was unable to defend the shieling grounds from the Scots and that his people were reluctant to venture out summering, 'which is their chiefest profitt' (Fraser 1971, 51).

The abolition of the practice of summering was in part a gradual process brought about by the expansion of permanent settlement into the uplands. Its long-term survival since the early Middle Ages reflects not only its economic viability but also with what difficulty change came to this isolated area, so long devastated by wars and raiding. The final act that brought about the end of shielding may have been the result of Crown estate policy, since the Crown had long regarded transhumance as unsatisfactory in terms of revenue and defence against raids (Wrathmell 1975, 259). Shieling grounds in the more accessible regions were leased in preference to the shielings themselves, thus beginning the process of dismantling customary tenure that had tied the population down to the manor for so long. Some shielings evolved into permanently settled farmsteads in the seventeenth century, and farms such as Shield-on-the-Wall and Steel Rigg may have begun life in such a way. The latest evidence for the occupation of shielings comes from Shiels Brae, in the valley of the White Lyne, Cumbria, where a clay pipe of 1650–70 was discovered. It is unlikely that shielings were still being built at this time, but the date is very close to the founding of the first permanent settlements in the upland areas of Northumberland and Cumberland (Ramm *et al.* 1970, 6). The change from seasonal to permanent settlement is the subject of the next chapter.

PLATE 1 *Building the Roman Wall* from the history of Northumbria paintings by William Bell Scott at Wallington Hall (The National Trust). The model for the centurion was John Clayton, the nineteenth-century landowner and archaeologist responsible for rescuing the Wall from piecemeal destruction (National Trust Photographic Library / A. C. Cooper).

PLATE 1

PLATE 2 The National Trust Hadrian's Wall estate, Northumberland, looking east from Steel Rigg towards Housesteads Fort. People have been living and working in this seemingly barren landscape for thousands of years (© AirFotos 1996).

(*Opposite*)
PLATE 3 In 1848 the artist T. M. Richardson walked the length of the Wall in the company of John Collingwood Bruce, the leading Wall scholar of his day. His watercolours show the Roman remains either before or just after Clayton had begun his excavations: *above* Milecastle 39, better known as Castle Nick; *below* The Vallum near Shield-on-the-Wall Farm (Estate of C. M. Daniels).

PLATE 2

PLATE 3

PLATE 4

PLATE 5 View from Housesteads Fort towards Beggar Bog, showing the consolidated walls of the *praetorium* or headquarters building in the foreground. The exposed Roman remains reveal little of the history of later occupation, such as the Tudor farmstead and seventeenth-century bastle house (National Trust Photographic Library / Paul Wakefield).

(*Opposite*)
PLATE 4 The north gate of Milecastle 37 during excavations in 1989. Here the late Roman blocking has been removed, revealing the finely tooled stone of the original gateway beneath. Despite almost 150 years of research, archaeology still has a great deal to tell us about the building and occupation of Hadrian's Wall (C. Dixon).

PLATE 5

PLATE 6 The Clayton Wall on Cuddy's Crags. The appearance of today's landscape probably owes more to
the work of Clayton and his successors than to the Romans. One hundred and fifty years ago the Wall would have
been little more than a pile of rubble, many fields were under the plough and few trees punctuated the skyline
(National Trust Photographic Library / David Noton).

PLATE 6

PLATE 7 The living landscape. Thousands of years of human occupation has influenced a rich habitat for fauna and flora. The exposed crags of the Whin Sill at Peel Gap (above) are home to bird cherry and wheatear, whilst the raised bogs contain few-flowered sedge and large heath butterfly, as well as evidence for Bronze Age use predating the bog (National Trust Photographic Library / Charlie Waite).

PLATE 7

PLATE 8 A calm day at Crag Lough. Today's visitors are more likely to battle against wind and rain than Roman auxiliaries or Border reivers. Nonetheless, this sparsely populated part of England retains the atmosphere of a wild and contested frontier. World Heritage Site status, together with the work of the National Trust, ensures the protection of this extraordinary historic landscape (National Trust Photographic Library / Charlie Waite).

PLATE 8

5

FROM REIVERS TO FARMERS

All the wild country along each side of the Roman Wall from Walltown to Walwick has been immemorially celebrated as the fastness of gangs of thieves, till their sanctuary of cruelty and rapine was finally invaded by the Military Road that made through it in the middle of the last century.

(Hodgson 1840)

The Border reivers

Hodgson's quotation neatly sums up the situation found throughout the area of the Hadrian's Wall estate between the sixteenth and eighteenth centuries. The post-medieval period was characterised by the violent struggle between England and Scotland and the raids carried out by the infamous Border reivers. In 1286 Edward I moved his armies northwards in an attempt to assert his suzerainty over the Scots and so began three centuries of conflict between England and Scotland that was to end only with the Union of the Crowns in 1603. Warfare, the devastation of the Black Death in the fourteenth century, and the everyday struggle to survive in the marginal lands of south-west Northumberland brought about a society regarded as being outside that of the rest of the country, and the Border land on both sides of the frontier became a byword for lawlessness, Godlessness, poverty and death. During the thirteenth and fourteenth centuries the region witnessed a number of major invasions and reprisals, but it is debatable how far this affected the isolated farms and shieling grounds of the middle lengths of the Wall. In the fifteenth and sixteenth centuries, however, there was a change in the pattern of conflicts from one of distinct major events often orchestrated by the powers in London and Edinburgh to a more continuous phase of small-scale raids and skirmishes across the Border and amongst the Border families, between whom feuding was a way of life.

The Roman Wall ran through an area known as the Middle March, which was under the command of a Warden responsible for the defence of the area from raiders and for suppressing and arresting reivers from his own March who had encroached into the other country (Fraser 1971, 129). His job was nigh on impossible, and in 1541 a survey was carried out by Bowes and Ellerker to assess the condition of the Border strongholds in the Middle March and provide recommendations for improving defence (reproduced in Hodgson 1828, 239 ff.). Orders were issued that two watchmen be kept nightly in every township on the borders of the Middle March on pain of a fine of 6s 8d to 'give warning of any outcry or cause of fray in the country'. Watchers were to be placed along the line of the Wall at 'Hautwysle Burnhead upon Caw-cragg in Hautwysle field' and between the 'Caw-gap and Knag-burn head' (Hodgson 1840, 118). A further survey in 1552 recommended that two men from each of the villages of Thorngrafton, Henshaw and Melkridge keep watch on the Wall 'from the King's Hill to the Craw-cragge'. The township of Haltwhistle was similarly to provide two men to keep watch of the 'Crow-cragge' (Hodgson 1840, 118–19). Indeed, the reuse of the Wall to defend the March seemed to appeal to one anonymous writer (possibly Lord Hunsdon, Warden of the East March between 1577 and 1594), who in 1587 proposed to Elizabeth I that the Wall be rebuilt to prevent the 'dayly and daungerous incurtyons of the valyaunte barberous Scottyshe nation'. The cost he proposed for the work was estimated at £30,000, a price too high for the Queen, and the project was never begun (Birley 1961, 23–4). Protection was most effectively safeguarded, however, by remaining loyal to the most powerful lord or clan in the district and the payment to them of extortion money or livestock.

The Border economy

Everyday life for the inhabitants of the Borders was lived under the constant shadow of raiding, either by the Scots or by a rival English family. The most infamous Border clan were the Armstrongs who, along with other minor families such as the Elliots, would ride out from their lair in Liddesdale and pass through the Busy Gap on their way to raid English settlements in Tynedale. The most powerful English family in the region were the Ridleys. From their seat at Willimoteswick south of the Tyne, they grew wealthy on the land and gave their name to the township, which was divided into two parts, the upper part lying north of Hadrian's Wall in the area now known as Ridley Common. In an area dominated by raiders and landowners, agricultural settlement was mostly confined to the valley bottom around the villages of Thorngrafton, Henshaw and Melkridge, with Haltwhistle providing the major market in the region. The area's principal economy was stock-raising, with cattle predominating over sheep. Cattle were bred and raised to be sold to farms in the south, where they were fattened and sold for beef. Numerous drove roads (unmetalled tracks used to move livestock from Scotland to the South) are known in the region, including one that runs past Steel Rigg and Once Brewed down to Henshaw and beyond. Sheep were pastured on the uplands and were mainly kept for wool rather than mutton, and one or two horses were kept for transport. An average farmer or statesman, the northern equivalent of a yeoman, could make a moderate living from 6 to 9 head of cattle, 2 horses and 20 to 40 sheep. Goats and chickens may also have been kept for milk and eggs. The income could be subsidised by mining, quarrying and cottage handcraft industries (Thirsk 1969,

22). The area was unsuitable for arable farming and produced only a meagre corn harvest; the staple diet of the inhabitants was barley or bigg (a poorer and hardier variety of barley), and oats. Hay was cut for animal fodder. Poor harvests caused by bad weather and political upheaval led to food shortages and supplies had to be brought in from abroad, most notably rye from Gdansk in Poland. In the 1590s aid failed to arrive and the region was stricken by famine, plague and cattle sickness. The same sequence of misfortunes followed again in 1622, 1623 and 1629 (Thirsk 1969, 20).

The upland areas of the Tyne valley lay largely unenclosed until the late seventeenth century; there were few hedges, no plantations or copses, no drained loughs, no stone walls and no defined roads except the already grassed-over Stanegate and Military Way (Storey 1973, 26). Bastle houses were characteristic of sixteenth- and seventeenth-century settlement throughout the Border lands of Northumberland and Cumberland, and are known at Housesteads and Bradley Green, as well as at Grandy's Knowe and Bradley Hall (Figure 30). They were typically rectangular in plan with thick stone walls and consisted of two storeys. The lower storey, known as the byre, was used for housing livestock at night to protect the animals from raiders, whilst the family lodged upstairs, a feature unique in Britain (Ramm *et al.* 1970, 61). Access to the living-quarters was by a stone staircase on the outside of the building. Some of the larger bastles had an overhanging battlement above the family room: if the bastle was attacked, the defenders could position themselves here and cast down hot water, arrows and stones, as this late seventeenth-century description shows:

> The county of Northumberland hath been exceedingly infested with the thieving of
> cattle, which is the remains of the Border Trade. This was so great a mischief that all the

FIGURE 30 Artist's impression of a bastle house. Buildings such as these are known throughout Northumberland, as well as Cumbria and the Scottish Borders. Of those that survive, most are now derelict or have been incorporated into later farm buildings. (Northumberland National Park)

considerable farmhouses were built of stone in the manner of a square tower, with an overhanging battlement, and, underneath, the cattle were lodged for the night. In the upper room the family lodged, and when the alarm came, they went up to the top and, with hot water and stones from the battlements, fought in defence of their cattle. (North 1742, 138)

The Union of the Crowns in 1603 may have resolved the political divisions between England and Scotland but did not immediately bring peace to the area, which remained a region of banditry and poverty well into the late seventeenth century. Housesteads became the lair of scurrilous horse thieves and free passage throughout the Borders was impossible without an armed escort. During the reign of Charles II the area was visited by the Lord Chancellor, Francis North, having been armed by the Sheriff of Northumberland for the journey. Writing in 1742, North's grandson Roger gave a vivid picture of life in the Border country:

> The Northumberland Sheriff gave us all arms; that is a Dagger, Knife, Penknife, and Fork, all together. And all because the hideous road along by the Tyne, for the many sharp turnings and perpetual precipices, was for a coach, not sustained by main force, impassable. His Lordship was forced to take Horse, and to ride most part of the way. (North 1742, 139)

Of the road to Hexham, Roger noted that:

> His lordship saw the true image of a Border country. The tenants of the several manors are bound to guard the judges through their precinct; and out of it they would not go an inch, to save the souls of them. They were a comical sort of people, riding on negs, as they called their small horses, with long beards, cloaks, and long broad swords, with basket hilts, hanging in broad belts that their legs and swords almost touched the ground; and every one in his turn, with his short cloak, and other equipage, came up cheek by jowl, and talked with my lord judge. His lordship was very pleased with their discourse; for they were great antiquarians in their own grounds. (North 1742, 140)

Francis North and his party arrived in Carlisle in about 1680, their journey being 'most pleasant and direct; and bating Hunger and Thirst, which will not be quenched by anything to be fastened upon, but which the Bounty of the Shire affords'. It would appear that, even in the late seventeenth century, Tynedale remained as desolate and sparsely populated, not to mention dangerous, as it had been since the fourteenth century.

Housesteads as a Border stronghold

At the centre of this zone of lawlessness lay Housesteads, home to a branch of the notorious Armstrong clan, described by North as being 'a great nuisance in the county, frightening people in their houses, and taking what they liked' (1742, 139). The earliest reference to Housesteads in the post-medieval period is contained in the schedule of the Border Watch, set out in the Border Survey of 1541. There it is stated that two watchmen were to be stationed between Caw Gap and Knagburne

Head, presumably the valley of the Knag Burn immediately east of Housesteads. The name 'House Steads' first appears later in the sixteenth century, when it was in the hands of Nicholas Crane of Bradley Hall, but it also appears as 'Chester in the Wall near Busygap'. In 1568 Hugh Crawhawe (Crowhall) held Housesteads along with many other properties in Thorngrafton township, including Bradley Hall, Crindledykes and Crowhall itself. These or similar properties were settled on his daughter as part of a marriage settlement in 1615; and in 1629 one George Nixon acquired a long lease at Housesteads from Hugh Crowhall (NRO 2219.70). Further references to the Nixons can be found in the Haltwhistle parish records. The farmland at Housesteads was subdivided between a number of tenants, and explicitly described as such by Nick Gibson in 1629: 'intermixing dale by dale with a tenement' (NRO 2219.70). The existence of two tenancies later in the seventeenth century, both held by members of the Armstrong clan, is demonstrated by documents of that date preserved amongst the Clayton deeds at Northumberland Records Office (NRO 2219.70).

In 1604 another resident of Housesteads, Hugh Nixon, was recorded as a stealer of cattle and a receiver of stolen goods in the Lord Howard's Household Books for the Dacre estates around Gilsland (Ornsby 1878, 445). Later in the century the activities of the Armstrongs gave the site a fearsome reputation. Established at the nearby bastle farmstead at Grandy's Knowe, the family are also recorded as tenants and briefly as freeholders at Housesteads from 1663 onwards (NRO 2219.70). They operated as horse-stealers, ranging as far north as Perth and as far south as the Midlands (Bosanquet and Birley 1955, 168). Evidently horse-stealing was insufficiently lucrative since the family were mortgaged up to the hilt from 1688 onwards. Although Nicholas was able to purchase the freehold of his farm in 1692, Thomas and William sold their holding to John Mitchelson in 1694. Nicholas finally gave up the struggle in 1698, and in that year both tenements were then purchased by Thomas Gibson of Hexham (NRO 2219.70). Gibson seems to have had an agreeable relationship with the Armstrongs as they stayed on as tenants until 1704, the year William Lowes of Hotbank gave evidence against Nicholas Armstrong for stealing sheep from Hotbank Common. Nicholas was hanged for his crimes and his two brothers emigrated to America. It is interesting to note that two years previously Nicholas Armstrong had given evidence against William Lowes for his alleged part in the assault on William Turner of Crindledykes, who aided in the apprehension of a relative of the Armstrong brothers (Hodgson 1840, 334–5). This turn of events highlights the level of violence and crime and the desire for revenge in this untamed corner of England.

The sixteenth- and seventeenth-century settlement at Housesteads consisted of a bastle house in front of the south gate of the fort on the south face of the east guard chamber, which was incorporated as a second ground-floor room (Figure 31). The ground-floor entrance lies mid-way along the sidewall, a feature it shares with bastles at Bradley Green and Grandy's Knowe near by. The ground-floor doorway is on the west side and the door mouldings are quite distinct from Roman work. The ground floor has a number of narrow loop windows including one cut through the masonry of the guard chamber, which formed a second room on the ground floor. In the narrow loop south of the doorway is part of a Roman window head used as the bottom sill. The upper floor was reached on the east side, where steps gave access across the outer wall, and a separate, probably later set of steps is located near the south-east corner. A second possible bastle can be identified in the south-east angle of the fort. A sizeable longhouse, much larger in plan than the bastle houses, lies across the *via principalis* (main thoroughfare), straddling the south entrance and is probably broadly contemporary with the bastle houses. Bosanquet

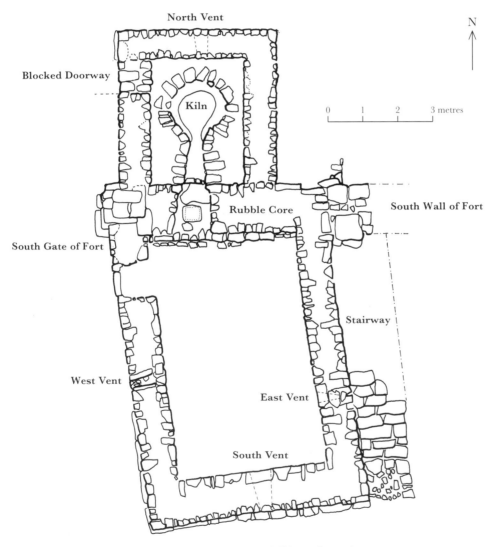

FIGURE 31 Plan of Housesteads bastle house. (After Whitworth 1990)

recorded that a 'seventeenth-century farmhouse' overlay the south-west corner of Building XI and the south-east angle of Barrack VI and is probably the predecessor of the later eighteenth-century farmhouse that lay further to the north, over the hospital (Bosanquet 1904, 198, 239). Ridge and furrow running down the slope from the fort may date from this period and there is no reason to doubt that the banditry that occupied Housesteads at this time may have practised some sort of cereal cultivation to subsidise their thieving enterprises. A corn-drying kiln, built from re-used Roman stone, lies in the south gate east guard-chamber, which had formed the north chamber of the bastle. The bastle cannot have been in use at this time but the kiln may have been associated with the longhouse, and a seventeenth-century date for the kiln is not impossible. It was only when the site was reoccupied by the Gibson family that Housesteads was to be connected with the more peaceful activity of farming.

Farmsteads and field enclosure

The years of the Border reivers devastated Tynedale, leaving it politically, economically and socially well behind the rest of the country. By the sixteenth century, the medieval system of feudalism had rapidly been broken down to be replaced by a more centralised authority throughout most of the country. This brought about the enclosure of previously open fields and extensive land improvement and by the middle of the seventeenth century most of lowland England was enclosed. The uplands of south-west Northumberland, however, remained largely uninhabited, except for a few scattered bastle houses and seasonally occupied shielings, but the following 150 years saw dramatic changes that would permanently transform the nature of the landscape.

North of Peel Crags, between Steel Rigg car-park and Crag Lough, lies a system of field enclosures associated with ridge and furrow. It is thought that this represents the earliest evidence for permanent non-defended settlement of the upland marginal areas since the fourteenth century. Evidence throughout the region indicates a gradual expansion of settlement around the late seventeenth century and the establishment of individual farmsteads. At first sight, this does not seem to have been the most opportune moment for such a development: the climate was no better than in the previous century, the land was still in the grip of the 'Little Ice Age', which continued to 1850, and the area was still ravaged by banditry and violence. The country had, however, been through a period of readjustment after the Civil War and the Restoration of the Monarchy which may have led to changes in population and agricultural practice. During the Civil War, a number of prominent landowners lost their land, most notably the Ridleys of Willimoteswick, who sided with the Royalists and whose land was subsequently confiscated by Cromwell. Other landowners were able to buy back their property but the Willimoteswick Ridleys were alone in losing almost all their land, which was granted by Parliament to the Nevils of Chevet, Yorkshire. The Nevils entered into articles of agreement with their tenants, but failed to manage their newly acquired land properly, having little interest in the apparently barren uplands of Tynedale (Hodgson 1840, 341).

The Nevils eventually sold their land both directly and indirectly to the Blackett family of Matfen sometime between 1673 and 1675. The land around Haltwhistle, known as the 'West Water estate', included the old seat of the Ridleys at Willimoteswick, together with the tithes of Haltwhistle and the lordship of several townships, including Thorngrafton, Ridley, Henshaw, Melkridge and Haltwhistle (NRO ZBL). Sir William Blackett, 1st Baronet of Matfen, was a member of a new class of landowning gentry who owed their rise to the industrial and commercial activity associated with the coal trade. Another new landowner, William Colesworth, the son of a Teesdale yeoman, rose through coal and salts to possession of agricultural estates near Haltwhistle around this time (Thirsk 1975, 43). Men such as these brought about the end of customary tenure, the practice whereby the tenure of a piece of land was passed down through the generations, and initiated the establishment of leaseholds, replacing small fixed dues with rents that could be revised periodically in accordance with changes in the value of agricultural produce. It had been this change which had seen the end of seasonal shieling in the uplands, transforming a way of life that had existed for hundreds of years. The conversion to leasehold tenure allowed a substantial increase in the value of tenements and the capital raised was reinvested in land improvements. One of the most striking aspects of the latter was the enclosure of open fields and common pasture, and their subsequent division into smaller areas, each allocated to an individual farmhouse (Wrathmell 1975, 191). The exact date for the establishment of these new farmsteads varies between regions and individual settlements. A decree of Charles II dated 1666 concerning tenements in the Manor of Henshaw mentions a Thomas Ridley of 'The Bogg', the original name of East Bog (NRO 309/2/4) and the first records for other farms in the region also date from the late seventeenth to early eighteenth century, eg Hotbank in 1698, High Shield in 1700.

Steel Rigg Farm

The remains of the original farm at Steel Rigg can be seen lying north of Peel Crags in what is now known as Hotbank West End. It is marked on the 1749 Allgood version of the proposed Military Road map as a farmstead surrounded by a number of enclosed fields lying within an area of open, unenclosed land (Figure 32). Other enclosed fields are known from the Allgood map and, although the latter is not accurate, it clearly indicates farmed land as opposed to open pasture. The area is also marked on the 1783 Henshaw Township Enclosure Award map and is specifically noted as being 'anciently inclosed land' (NRO 309/m. 71) (Figure 33) (see pp. 82–3 for a discussion of enclosure). A lease agreement of 1698 between the

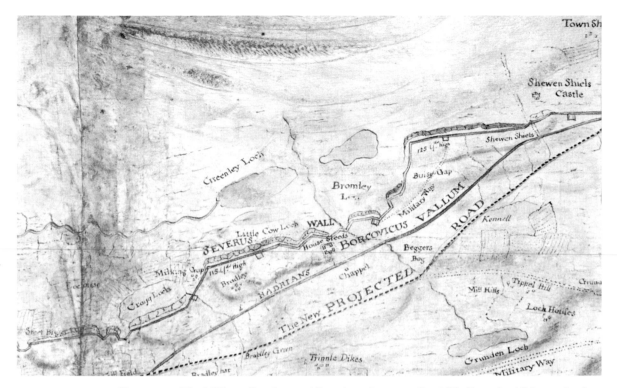

FIGURE 32 The Military Road map, Allgood version, 1751. Steel Rig Farm is visible north of the Wall. The boundaries on the map are roughly traceable on the ground today. The Military Road (now the B6318) still follows this course. (Society of Antiquaries of Newcastle)

owner Sir Edward Blackett, Baronet, and the leaseholder, William Lowes of Crowhall, provides a description of Steel Rigg Farm:

> that part of Moor ground situated within the Lordship of Henshaw and known by the name of Steele alias Steele Rigg, lying on the north side of the Roman or Pict Wall and bordering on the south by the same Pict Wall. [The boundary] on the west [lies] on a highway between Henshaw and Saughy Rig, and on the north on a burn below Hounds Hill. [The boundary] on the east [lies] on a tenancy now in the possession of the said William Lowes alias Lough Head. [Leased] together with all lands, grounds, foodings, domains, pastures and shooting rights ... also all mines and minerals and quarries of coal, stones and quartz found within the same tenancy. (NRO ZBL 1/100)

The remains of Steel Rigg Farm consist of a number of earthwork banks, collapsed boulder walls, and relics of stone-clad banks (Figure 34). Narrow ridge and furrow can be seen on the Steel Rigg and on the bank opposite to the north. The walls and hedges were used to separate livestock from the crops. On the south-facing bank opposite Steel Rigg are the remains of what may have been the farmhouse. There is a banked enclosure divided into two halves, the larger part probably being a yard, the other the house itself. Another possible building lies to

manner of ears of corn and grain shall be grown … with all manner of grass' (NRO ZBL 1/100). Oats and bigg may also have been grown, as perhaps were potatoes (Thirsk, 1975, 30). Corn-drying kilns are known from Housesteads and Bradley Green and are characteristic of this period, but none are known from Steel Rigg. Also associated with the farm is a large circular enclosure thought to be a stack stand, the purpose of which was to provide a fairly level, dry platform on which to pile a stack of winter fodder and to afford protection for the latter from animals. Other examples are known north of Housesteads Fort (Ramm *et al.* 1970, 54). Cattle and sheep, however, would have formed the mainstay of the agricultural economy, with cattle used for milking and sheep predominantly for mutton rather than wool (although no doubt the latter was a factor in the local economy), and the sheep may well have been milked (Thirsk 1975, 31).

The first records referring to Cawfields Farm come from an Abstract of title deeds dated 1673 when William Carr and his wife Mary sold the lease on to Hugh Coulson (NRO ZBL 290). Cawfields Farm probably resembled other early farmsteads in the region with a linear farmhouse surrounded by hedges or drystone boundaries. Ridge and furrow is known north of the Wall from aerial photographs and corn and grain were probably grown, and livestock grazed on the surrounding land. Cawfields lies to the very north of Haltwhistle Township on Haltwhistle Common or Fell and whilst the lower part of the township in the Tyne valley was formally enclosed by private agreement in the eighteenth century, the upper part lay open and remained common land until the nineteenth century. The Enclosure Award map of the Manor of Melkridge dated 1793 (NRO 309/m. 89) notes that landowners exchanged land 'for stints in Cawfields', meaning that they had grazing rights on Cawfields Common, the land between the Roman Wall and the Military Road. The moor was finally enclosed in 1844 but Cawfields Common remained unenclosed for pasture. This late enclosure and the lack of later agricultural activity probably ensured the survival not only of the Vallum but also of the Roman camps alongside the Haltwhistle Burn. The original pre-Enclosure Act field boundaries still survive north of the crags, as seen in the 1840 Tithe Map.

Other farms on the estate reveal similar characteristics but only at Steel Rigg does the evidence survive so well (Figure 36). The 1749 Allgood version of the Military Road map indicates that the land south of Hadrian's Wall was partly enclosed and marks the farmsteads known as 'Peel' (Peel Bothy), 'Black Bank' (East Bog) and, further to the east, 'Milking Gap' (Hotbank) and Highshields. The 1793 Enclosure Award map of the Manor of Henshaw highlights 'anciently inclosed land' not only at Steel Rigg but also around Peel Cottage, East Bog and Highshield Farm. The fact that late eighteenth-century enclosure surveyors considered this land 'anciently inclosed' suggests not only that the farms were well established but also that some of the boundaries may already have gone out of use by this time. None the less, the remains of some of these boundaries can be seen running across the present-day East Bog and Bradley farms. These late seventeenth- to early

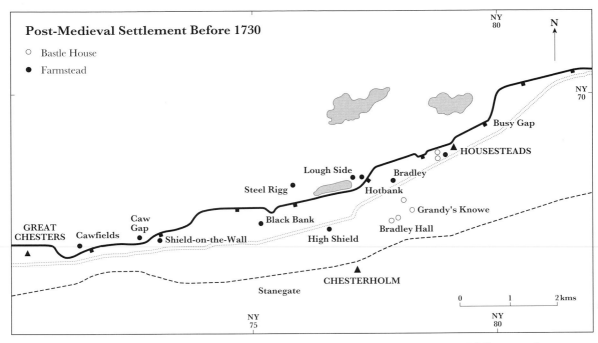

Post-Medieval Settlement Before 1730

N

○   Bastle House

●   Farmstead

Busy Gap

HOUSESTEADS

Lough Side

Bradley

Steel Rigg

Hotbank

Grandy's Knowe

Black Bank

Caw
Gap

Bradley Hall

GREAT
CHESTERS

Cawfields

Shield-on-the-Wall

High Shield

CHESTERHOLM

Stanegate

0   1   2 kms

FIGURE 36 Post-medieval settlement on the National Trust Hadrian's Wall estate, 1600–1730.

eighteenth-century boundaries differ from the later Enclosure period walls: they are often hedge banks (earth banks on which hedges were planted) or earth-packed dry-stone walls that pay closer attention to the topography, dividing the landscape into small allotments. The surrounding land, if not similarly enclosed by another farmstead, was commonly used for grazing. Extensive areas of narrow ridge and furrow can be seen north of Crag Lough on Hotbank Farm and around Cawfields, East Bog and Bradley farms. Enclosure did not itself change the quality of the land but was accompanied by improvements such as stone clearance, drainage, fertilisation, and new farmsteads and outbuildings (Wrathmell 1975, 195). The 1793 Enclosure Award map of the Manor of Henshaw is the earliest map to show a number of small properties in the vicinity of Peel Gap (see Figure 33).

It was during the late seventeenth to early eighteenth centuries that Housesteads was to emerge as a working farm and was occupied by the Gibson family from 1698 to 1838. The antiquary William Stukeley, who visited the site in 1725, provided a sketch which shows a farmhouse with a crosswing at its east end overlying the site of the hospital within the Roman fort. At some point in the later eighteenth century this farmhouse was removed and another built just outside the south entrance of the fort. The antiquary John Brand (1744–1806), who visited the site in 1779, recorded an altar being used as a mantelpiece in the farmhouse (Brand 1789, 610; Collingwood and Wright 1965, 504, 1586). The eighteenth century saw an intensification in land use and general agricultural improvement such as

FIGURE 37 Post-medieval corn-drying kiln built into the ruins of the granary at Housesteads Fort. The kiln probably dates to the early eighteenth-century farmstead recorded by Stukeley on his travels. (National Trust Photographic Library)

(*Opposite*)
FIGURE 38 Busy Gap and the King's Wicket earthwork, which is presumed to be early post-medieval, but appears to overlie evidence for ridge and furrow. The King's Wicket in fact refers to the wicket gate in the line of the drystone wall that lies on top of the Roman Wall. (Photo: T. Gates, 1992 © copyright reserved)

enclosure and drainage. The now-destroyed limekiln in the south-west corner of the farm probably dates from this period. Cereal cultivation was carried out and it is possible that the corn-drying kiln in the south granary of the fort may have replaced the one in the south gate (Figure 37). Fields of ridge and furrow were defined by hedges, representing the first moves towards enclosure and the separation of arable and pasture land. The completion of the Military Road in 1757 no doubt facilitated the agricultural improvement of adjoining farms and must have prompted a good deal of boundary readjustment or definition. The township of Thorngrafton was finally enclosed by an Act of Parliament in 1793 and marked the shift away from mixed farming practices to complete pasture. By the time John Clayton bought the farm in 1838 the grazing of livestock had become the predominant form of land use.

The Military Road

In 1745 the Jacobite Rebellion prompted the building of a new road between Newcastle and Carlisle. The English army had been bogged down just outside Hexham, unable to drag their heavy artillery over the difficult ground and in 1751 an Act of Parliament was passed to allow the building of a new road, known as The Military Road, that would allow easy passage between the two towns (Lawson 1966, 189). Previously, long journeys had been undertaken on foot and goods carried on packhorses along the line of the Stanegate, still in use at this time, or routes in the Tyne valley (Lee 1876, 50). The road was built almost entirely along the line of Hadrian's Wall, and is the most destructive act of

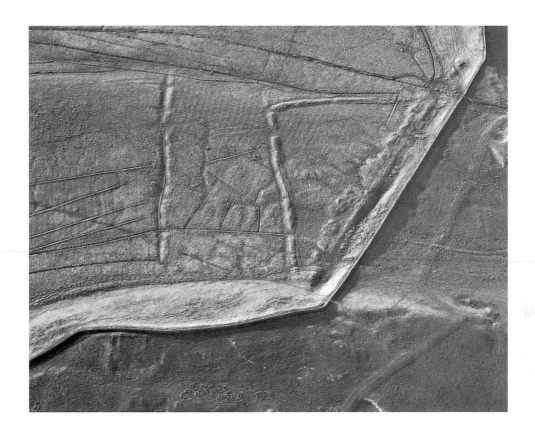

vandalism ever to have occurred to it. The line of the Wall in the estate was only preserved because of the topography (see Figure 32). Here, the road followed the line of the Vallum between Highshield Farm and Winshields, and numerous quarries are known along the side of the road, providing aggregate and building material. The road, built by General Wade, was completed by 1757. It increased access to the upland region, resulting in the establishment of new farms and a further expansion of settlement.

Despite being built for military purposes, the road was run on a commercial basis as a turnpike. Along its length, toll houses such as Bradley Barr, just west of the junction with the road running down to Bardon Mill past Bradley Hall, collected fees from travellers passing between Newcastle and Carlisle. Its location can still be seen today as an indent in the boundary wall north of the Military Road. The original Twice Brewed Inn, known as the Twice Brewed Ale and now East Twice Brewed farmhouse, dates from this time, providing simple accommodation for 'as many as twenty men and fifty horses on a carrier's night' (Bruce 1921, 178). William Hutton, the 78-year-old Quaker who walked the entire length of the Wall in 1801, complained about the unavailability of beds in the inn and was almost forced to share a couch with a carrier. That night 'fifteen carriers approached, each with one horse cart', who fed on beef and pudding, informing Hutton that eating was 'the chief end of man' (Hutton, 1802). Traffic also ran from north to south and the 'highway' mentioned in 1698 that acted as the western boundary of Steel Rigg Farm is thought to have been a drove road bringing cattle and sheep down from Scotland to the markets in the South. Another drove road is known from the east end of the estate running through Busy Gap, where the drovers built an earthwork stock enclosure known as the 'King's Wicket', after the gateway in the line of the Roman Wall, to pen the cattle in overnight (Figure 38).

The Enclosure Acts

By 1750, as the Allgood map suggests, the landscape of the estate was a patchwork of small farmsteads surrounded by swathes of open commonly grazed land. Writing in the mid-nineteenth century, John Clayton reveals that 'so late as the middle of the last century the lands on the north side of the Roman Wall, in this district, were uninclosed commons' (Clayton 1855a, 272). Clearly he was unaware of the earlier seventeenth-century enclosures that had surrounded the small upland farmsteads. Despite the fact that the process of enclosing the English countryside had been taking place since the sixteenth century, by 1700 it was estimated that 2,832,900 ha (7 million acres) of 'waste and common' remained to be enclosed (Hoskins 1955, 178). During the late eighteenth to early nineteenth centuries a series of Enclosure Acts was passed by Parliament whereby much of this land was enclosed by private agreement between landowners and tenants – for example, the Forest of Lowes and Hotbank Common in 1751 (NRO ZBL 4/19/1). Where land was owned predominantly by one landowner, such as Sir Edward Blackett on Hotbank Common, private agreement was straightforward, but where the land was divided between a number of different owners, problems arose. A glance at the 1793 Enclosure Map of Henshaw reveals a vast number of properties divided up between an equally large number of owners whose properties are scattered through the area (see Figure 33). In 1787 an Act of Parliament brought about the enclosure of Henshaw Township (NRO ZBL 268/1). Melkridge Township was also enclosed in this year (NRO QRD 7) and Thorngrafton in 1793 (NRO QRA 50). Haltwhistle Common, including land at Cawfields south of the Wall, was not enclosed until 1844 (NRO 691/1) and the Tithe Award map for that year (NRO 2588) reveals the landscape as it was prior to government enclosure.

The new field boundaries consisted of drystone walls made up of stone retrieved from field clearance or quarries. They were built according to the surveyed boundaries set out by the Acts of Parliament, often running up the hill at 90 degrees to the Military Road, taking little notice of the topography that had governed the layout of earlier divisions (see Figure 32). The landscape that had been slowly formed over the last 1,000 years or so was wiped away within years as farms expanded and farming practices changed. By 1844, the Tithe map for Henshaw Township reveals the new walls taking no account of the earlier enclosures, and the landscape begins to resemble its present-day state with self-contained farms centred on individual farmhouses and their outbuildings. There can be no doubt that the period of the Enclosure Acts caused the biggest impact on the landscape of the estate since the building of Hadrian's Wall almost 1,700 years earlier.

Wars with France 1793–1815

Between the time of the earliest Enclosure Acts and the mid-nineteenth century, the uplands of Northumberland were extensively ploughed to supplement an ailing economy. Almost quarter of a century of war with France and her allies (1793–1815) increased domestic demand for grain and raised prices, rents and land values to unprecedented levels (Stamper 1989, 40), and so land previously under pasture was brought into cultivation. Whilst some of the low-lying land along Hadrian's Wall had been ploughed since the establishment of the earliest farmsteads such as Steel Rigg, the long years of wars with France at the turn of the century saw more and more marginal land being taken in for cultivation. In almost every single field on the Hadrian's Wall estate there is some evidence of ridge and furrow, even on the steepest and least likely slopes, with only the rockier and most exposed uplands being left to pasture. In 1801, the traveller the Rev. John Skinner noted near Great Chesters a farmer 'in the fields with his reapers', one of the few contemporary accounts of cultivation in this region at this time (Skinner 1978, 40). Unlike medieval ridge and furrow, some of which can be seen in the remains of the abandoned medieval settlement at Bradley Green, late post-medieval ridge and furrow is narrower (up to only 5 m between furrows) and straighter, lacking the character-istic 'inverted-S' shape of earlier plough marks (Taylor 1975, 143). Most of the ridge and furrow on the estate lies comfortably within the Enclosure Act stone walls, firmly dating it to the turn of the nineteenth century.

Most in demand during the war years was corn, which was taken down into the Tyne valley to be ground into flour and then transported to the cities. Oats and bigg remained important to the local economy, as were potatoes, which were a staple for the local population. The quality of the crop was likely to be poor, however. The exposed hillsides, coupled with heavy rainfall and low-quality soils, were no place for cultivating crops, and there must have been many a failed harvest. Indeed, many fields may have been planted only once before being abandoned. Whilst the small farmsteads at one time may have been able to support themselves, additional demand on the land was unsustainable. The extent of surviving ridge and furrow on the estate, however, shows the determination, if not the desperation, of the local farmers to produce more food for their families and for sale. Following the end of the Napoleonic wars the demand for grain and thus the price of land fell and the cultivation of the uplands was abandoned, the land reverting to pasture. By the middle of the nineteenth century, the over-riding importance of livestock had seen an end to all arable farming along the Wall.

6

JOHN CLAYTON AND THE BIRTH
OF CONSERVATION

The man who undoubtedly had the greatest influence and gave the strongest encouragement for Roman Wall studies during the nineteenth century was John Clayton (Figure 39). Born in 1792, he lived for almost a century until his death in 1890, and was responsible not only for some of the earliest excavations at sites along the Wall but for the creation of much of the landscape seen in the National Trust's estate today. His tireless devotion to the Wall and the management of his estate ensured the survival of the antiquities found within its boundaries and provided resources for a generation of archaeological research. The protection of Hadrian's Wall was one of the first acts of deliberate archaeological conservation in the world.

The Chesters estate

In 1809 Clayton became an articled clerk in his father's Law firm and in 1832 succeeded to the head of what was, for the next 60 years, one of the largest legal practices in the north of England. Like his father before him, John Clayton was Town Clerk of Newcastle upon Tyne and between 1830 and 1840 he was partly responsible for the development of the city. Indeed, he was possibly the only developer not to go bankrupt. He is especially noted for his support of Richard Grainger's replanning and rebuilding of Newcastle and for the establishment of the Newcastle and Carlisle Railway, as well as the building of the Cattle Market. Clayton Street near the Central Station was named after him. From his country seat at Chesters, Clayton was able to use his resources to indulge in his passion for Roman remains. Chesters is the site of the fort of Cilurnum and from an early age Clayton developed a devotion for the Roman Wall and its antiquities. He was alarmed to discover during his walks along the Wall that it and the forts, milecastles and turrets were regarded as a convenient quarry by neighbouring landowners and farmers for building materials to use in their farmhouses, walls, outhouses, sheds and drains. An account of his life recalls that:

> To talk of preserving the Wall was useless as long as well-shaped, handy-sized stones, lay ready to the hand of the farmer, and the carting away of its stones went forward merrily. The great pity of it was that it was the best portions of the Wall which were removed in this fashion, for the labourers naturally preferred to take the stones that were breast high in the standing wall to the stooping and lifting them up from the ground into their carts. (Budge 1903, 6)

As with the National Trust some 60 years later, Clayton realised that the only means of ensuring the protection of the landscape was through direct ownership. His response was to systematically purchase farms along the Wall as they came on to the market. In 1834 he bought up Steel Rigg, Loughside and Foulbog as well as Hotbank, which he jointly owned with Robert Ingram MP (these properties together make up the present-day Hotbank Farm), which gave him ownership of the Wall from the Knag Burn to Steel Rigg. In 1838, after some considerable competition, he acquired Housesteads Farm, including the fort, for £6,900 from Thomas Gibson. Clayton continued his purchases with Cawfields in 1844 and in 1848 began excavating Milecastle 42 at Hole Gap. East Cawfields followed in 1873. Shield-on-the-Wall was bought in 1848 and East Bog, then known simply as The Bogg, was purchased along with Pasture House on the south side of the Military Road in 1851. Beggar Bog was bought in 1853. The newly acquired farms formed an 'archaeological park' dedicated to the preservation of the antiquities within it. It should be noted that Highshield and Bradley farms were never part of the Chesters estate and remained in the hands of the Blackett family via the Trevelyans of Wallington until purchased by the National Trust in 1972 and 1975 respectively.

FIGURE 39 John Clayton (1792–1890), landowner and antiquary. (Museum of Antiquities, University of Newcastle upon Tyne)

FIGURE 42 Shield-on-the-Wall Farm in 1997. The farmhouse was rebuilt in *c.*1860 on the lower ground to the south. The drip-moulds and mullioned windows are characteristic of the buildings erected by Clayton along the length of the Wall. (Photo: J. Crow, 1997)

the antiquary Dr John Collingwood Bruce as being deserted in 1867 and by 1898 it had been demolished, no doubt because of its proximity to the Wall, as was the farm building overlooking Caw Gap, which was in ruins in 1867 (Bruce 1867, 227–9). Other farmsteads, namely Foulbog, Loughside and Closeholme, whose locations are known from eighteenth-century Enclosure Award maps, were demolished or moved not because of their location in relation to the Wall but because during the early nineteenth century limited arable cultivation was abandoned in favour of permanent pasture. There was a drop in population levels in the area as people were attracted to employment in the industrial cities. Surviving farms expanded and land that in 1793 (the year of the Act of Parliament enclosing the townships of Henshaw and Melkridge) was divided up amongst a number of different owners was, by 1866, nucleated around a single farmstead. Land was needed for pasture and the large open fields created by the enclosure acts provided grazing for sizeable herds of cattle and flocks of sheep. The 1st Edition Ordnance Survey map of 1866 reveals that the land was being extensively drained to increase the amount available for use and improve grazing for livestock. Clayton, therefore, was able to couple excellent estate management with conservation, and was the first to recognise the importance of Hadrian's Wall in the context of its surroundings.

Industrial activity on the Hadrian's Wall estate

The Enclosure Acts of the late eighteenth and early nineteenth centuries were part of a larger movement throughout Britain towards greater agricultural exploitation and industrialisation. The demand for lime (used for agricultural improvement) and the quest for raw materials needed to supply limekilns and furnaces brought about a new phase of land use to the uplands of the South Tyne valley. The abundance of limestone that runs in belts throughout the estate, coupled with pockets of coal and ironstone, not to mention ample supplies of whinstone for later road and rail construction, made the uplands a prime area for mineral extraction and minor industrial activity, which have left enduring marks on the landscape.

The agricultural land improvement of the late eighteenth and early nineteenth centuries required not only enclosure and drainage but also liming to reduce the acidity of the soil. Vast numbers of limekilns were built throughout England, particularly between 1790 and 1810 to meet the demand caused by enclosure and the need to increase crop yields during the wars with France (Raistrick 1973, 70). Lime-burning had occurred on the estate since Roman times, indicated by the kiln at Housesteads used for builder's mortar (Crow 1995, 23–26), and later post-medieval kilns, known as 'sow kilns', which have been identified at Cawfields just south of the Stanegate (Jobey 1966, 2). In May 1760 Bishop Pococke wrote from Haltwhistle describing this type of kiln in use: 'they [the farmers] make here a small round pile of wood and place limestone round it, cover it with sods, set the wood on fire and supply fuel until it is sufficiently burnt and this commonly on the spot they want to manure' (Jobey 1966, 2).

The old type of limekilns seen within the estate today at Bradley Farm (Figure 43)

FIGURE 43 Bradley Farm limekiln. The pointed draw arch is typical of limekilns found in the region. Limestone and coal were placed in the hole in the top and drawn out of the bottom. The lime was later slaked and put to agricultural use. (Photo: J. Crow, 1997)

works to the Haltwhistle Burn is clearly marked on the 6-inch 1866 Ordnance Survey map (sheet LXXXIII) and the course of one is still visible today skirting around the edge of the quarry. This formed part of a larger network of tramways running down the side of the Haltwhistle Burn servicing a number of different industries from Cawfields to Haltwhistle itself. Just south of the Military Road the tramway passed a large limestone quarry and two now collapsed limekilns. Another limekiln on the west bank survives in better condition and was described as being 'old' in 1860. The tramway crosses the burn at several places, crossing a coalmine and two woollen mills, of which only a few walls survive, and on to the yards of the South Tyne Colliery and the South Tyne Brickworks. From here, the processed iron ore may have been put on to the Newcastle–Carlisle Railway for use elsewhere (Linsley pers comm). More quarrying is known to the south-east of the coal shaft in Shield-on-the-Wall Farm.

In 1902 the tramway was extended north of the Military Road to serve the Cawfields Whinstone Quarry which ran from that year until 1952. The narrow-gauge tramway followed the course of the earlier wagonway down the Haltwhistle Burn to Haltwhistle itself. The quarry removed a section of Hadrian's Wall from Burnhead cottage to Hole Gap, just west of Milecastle 42. The quarrying also destroyed what may have been a medieval building discovered by F. G. Simpson in 1907 (Simpson, G. 1976, 80). After work had ceased the spoil heaps from the iron-stone works were removed from their position in the middle of Cawfields Common and dumped in the quarry, which was later flooded. The tramway was dismantled at this time but survives as a low trackbed on the east side of the Haltwhistle Burn. Slumping of the steep ground above the tramway has partly covered it at one point and it is being heavily eroded by the burn at the north end. Some of the dismantled rails and sleepers have been built into a makeshift bridge over the burn.

The break-up of the Chesters estate

After Clayton's death in 1890 the estate was held by his family, Clayton dying unmarried with no heirs. Maintenance of the Wall and further archaeological investigation were carried out by the Chesters estate under the supervision of F. G. Simpson. However, gambling debts accumulated by Jack Clayton, John's nephew, brought the family close to bankruptcy and in 1929 the Chesters estate was put up for sale by auction. The sale catalogue describes the estate as 'one of the best known and most extensive domains in the County of Northumberland', covering an area of almost 8,094 ha (20,000 acres). The Wall estate was only part of Clayton's enormous holdings but it attracted an 'almost world-wide interest' because of the Roman remains. The farms along the Wall were sold to private individuals and the estate broken up. Housesteads Farm, however, despite 'including the most perfect station on Hadrian's Wall', was withdrawn from sale at £6,250 and a buyer not found. It would seem that the responsibility of caring for a world-renowned archaeological site was off-putting. However, on the 3rd January 1930 *The Times* announced that Housesteads Fort had been given by Mr J. M. Clayton to the National Trust (*Illustrated London News* 1930a). The gift also included lengths of the Wall from Milecastle 37 in the west to the Knag Burn gateway to the east. Housesteads Farm was eventually bought by Professor George Trevelyan of Wallington Hall, who in 1934 donated land to the National Trust for the building of the museum. Thereafter, the Trust sought gradually to acquire land along the line of Hadrian's Wall, mirroring Clayton's systematic purchasing of farms, and leading to the establishment of the present-day Hadrian's Wall estate.

A threat to the Wall

Quarrying had been an important activity in the area of the estate since Roman times, but was relatively small scale for extracting either lime or building stone for houses, farm buildings and drystone walls. It had left its scar on the belts of limestone that run east to west on both sides of the Wall at Bradley Farm, Cawfields, Hotbank and elsewhere, but its impact on the archaeological remains was relatively low. Quarrying on a commercial basis, however, posed the biggest threat to Hadrian's Wall and the landscape in which it lay. In 1930, three months after it had been announced that Housesteads had been donated to the National Trust, plans were drawn up to start quarrying the Whin Sill from Shield-on-the-Wall eastwards to Housesteads (*Illustrated London News* 1930b). After the break-up of the Chesters estate in 1929, land including Shield-on-the-Wall and Hotbank farms had been bought up by Mr J. Wake of Darlington, who proposed to extract 200,000 tons of Whinstone a year for road building from Shield-on-the-Wall. The proposals created controversy almost immediately. Haltwhistle at that time was recorded as being among the four most deprived towns in Britain and the promise of the creation of 500 new jobs seemed to outweigh the benefits of conservation. However, such was the outcry made by the archaeological and political establishment of the day that Mr Wake was restrained from quarrying the line of the Wall itself and began blasting to the south, just north of the farmhouse. Part of the Military Way running up from Caw Gap was destroyed at this time. Pressure from the Establishment led to a conference which helped pass legislation to strengthen the Ancient Monuments Act that had been passed in 1929. The new law was passed by Parliament in 1931. Quarrying ceased at Shield-on-the-Wall and Mr Wake sold Hotbank Farm to the National Trust in 1942, but only a government order and costly compensation stopped the quarrying at Walltown to the west in 1943. Quarrying, however, continued at Cawfields and its termination in 1952 finally marked the end of industrial activity along the middle lengths of Hadrian's Wall.

The acquisition of Hotbank Farm gave the National Trust ownership of Housesteads Fort, Milecastles 37 and 39, and the entire length of the Wall from the Knag Burn gateway to Steel Rigg. The 1930s witnessed a flurry of archaeological activity at Housesteads and along the line of the Wall with excavations carried out by the Durham University Excavation Committee. By 1935 visitor numbers had reached 15,000 per year and the site was visited by HM Queen Mary. This momentum of research and public interest came to an end with the outbreak of the Second World War, which brought about wide social and economic changes throughout the nation that were reflected even at Housesteads.

A new role

Until the outbreak of the Second World War the National Trust was primarily seen as an organisation concerned with open-space property, such as the fells of the Lake District, but the decline in the fortunes of many of the owners of historic houses, especially during the war years, brought about the introduction of the Trust's 'Country-House Scheme'. The Trust's primary post-war role was to become the guardian of the English country house. In accordance with this many of its major archaeological properties were given into the care and guardianship of the Ministry of Works, which was deemed to be a body with greater expertise in the management of archaeological sites. Housesteads and the line of the Wall down to the Knagburn gateway came under guardianship in 1951, a move welcomed by many leading Wall scholars, including Ian Richmond and Eric Birley.

FIGURE 45 Ministry of Works workmen repairing the Wall at Willowford Bridge in 1957, demonstrating the lack of archaeological attention that so distressed the writer Jacquetta Hawkes. (Museum of Antiquities, University of Newcastle upon Tyne)

The methods employed to preserve Hadrian's Wall subsequently became a matter of contention. The National Trust, as inheritors of the Chesters estate, maintained the methods of preserving the Clayton Wall as set out by John Clayton and later by F. G. Simpson, whereby the original Roman material was left *in situ* and protected by building up the facing walls with drystone blocks and sealing the top with a turf cap. The Ministry, however, adopted a different approach and sought to consolidate walls and buildings *as found* with no new stonework added and restoration kept to an absolute minimum and recognisable for what it was. It was generally assumed by the Ministry that it would eventually take responsibility for the entire length of the Wall, a view not accepted by the Trust, and in 1957 a row broke out concerning the two methods of Wall conservation. The case for the National Trust was unofficially taken up by Jacquetta Hawkes, archaeologist, journalist and wife of the novelist J. B. Priestley. She visited the Wall in the winter of 1958 and wrote an article in *The Observer* attacking the Ministry's methods of consolidation. Mrs Hawkes was alarmed at the presentation of the consolidated Wall and the means by which work was carried out without the supervision of an archaeologist. It was clear to Mrs Hawkes that 'repairs and alterations were destroyed without record' and that the Wall that emerged from the consolidation was 'not Hadrian's Wall at all. It is a copy – and one that has lost all the gifts of time' (Figure 45). Her comments attracted widespread attention and questions were raised in the House of Commons. The Ministry was unrepentant, and it was to be nearly 25 years before archaeologists were employed to observe and record the Roman Wall during consolidation, a welcome return to the professional standards set by the Chesters estate and F. G. Simpson in the years before the First World War. The National Trust has maintained Clayton's and Simpson's methods of preserving the Clayton Wall, and has only used consolidation techniques, under the supervision of an archaeologist, on newly excavated sections of Wall, such as that between Castle Nick and Highshield Crags in the 1980s.

During the 1970s the Trust's Hadrian's Wall holdings expanded considerably. In 1972 Highshield Farm was donated to the National Trust, bringing the Vallum on both sides of the Military Road from East Twice Brewed to Bradley Farm into the estate and improving access to Castle Nick. Housesteads Farm was purchased from the Trevelyan family in 1974, giving the Trust ownership of the *vicus* outside the guardianship area. Bradley Farm followed the next year, improving public access to the south side of the Wall, as well as ownership of Milecastle 38 and a section of the Vallum. East Bog Farm was bought up in two parts between 1979 and 1983, with land bought from East Twice Brewed added to the East Bog tenancy in 1982. In 1987 Shield-on-the-Wall Farm was purchased and the land between East Bog and the Knag Burn began to be known as the 'old estate'. The 'new' estate was expanded in 1992 by the acquisition of Cawfields Farm with its finely preserved length of Vallum, marching camps, Military Way and Stanegate.

7

THE WALL REDISCOVERED

The ruins are sufficiently copious to attract the use of pickaxe and spade – an attention they will probably soon receive.

(Bruce 1863)

Hadrian's Wall has fascinated antiquaries, archaeologists and visitors for over 400 years. The eighteenth century in particular saw a rise in interest in the actual remains of the past, not just classical literature, and the Grand Tour of Europe became part of every wealthy young gentleman's education. The classical world of the Greeks and Romans influenced art, architecture, literature and law, and the discovery of Roman remains in Britain confirmed belief that this country had once been part of that distant and imperial past. No wonder William Stukeley called Housesteads the 'Tadmur of Britain' after the ruined city of Palmyra recently discovered in the Syrian desert. Britain was now the new Rome.

The construction of the Military Road along the line of much of the Wall in the 1750s, so deplored by Stukeley, meant studies became focused on the middle sections, nowhere more so than between Sewingshields and Cawfields. Housesteads without doubt drew the most attention and generations of archaeologists have dug and surveyed here – and even today there is more to be learnt about the fort and *vicus*. The rest of the Wall, along with the milecastles, turrets, ditch and Vallum, has also had its champions and the names of the men and women who have worked there reads like an archaeological hall of fame. Their ideas and perceptions of the Wall and the landscape have helped shape how they have been managed and conserved. Tomorrow's archaeologists will no doubt change our ideas once more.

First steps along the Wall

Antiquarian interest in Hadrian's Wall began in the sixteenth century with the publication of William Camden's *Britannia*, the first edition of which appeared in 1586. Camden, however, did not visit the Wall until 1599 and even then was prevented from investigating the middle lengths for 'fear of the rank robbers there-abouts' (Figure 46). Housesteads and the surrounding countryside remained in the grip of banditry during the seventeenth century and were off limits for visiting gentlemen scholars. However, a new edition of *Britannia* published by Gibson in 1695 aroused fresh interest in the Wall. This happened to coincide with the sale of

Housesteads to Thomas Gibson in 1698 and, despite the fact that the notorious Armstrong brothers appear to have remained there as tenants until 1704, the site was visited by Christopher Hunter in 1702. Hunter, in a letter published in *Philosophical Transactions*, the journal of the Royal Society, wrote: 'we came at the Housesteads, 'tis a ground adjoining upon Hadrian's or the Roman Wall, which is for a considerable space covered with the Ruins of houses destroy'd, among which I found several pedestals' (Hunter 1702, 1131). Hunter was unique in his day for referring to *Hadrian's* Wall and not Severus's Wall or the Pict Wall, as was the norm. He described it as being 'two yards [1.8 m] thick at least, and as I was told has been defended by a square tower at every mile, on the inside of the wall ... At some distance within the wall is a large double ditch, a single one without' (Hunter 1702, 1131; Rogan 1954, 122).

Over the next 30 years Housesteads saw a steady stream of visitors. Most antiquaries were interested only in inscriptions and sculptures, but some did provide descriptions of the course of the Wall. Robert Smith visited in 1708–9 to check and illustrate comments made on the Wall by the Venerable Bede who, in his work *A History of the English Church and People*, described it as being 'eight feet [2.4 m] in bredth, and twelve [3.7] in height' (Bede 1969, 52). Smith provided the first reasoned description of the Wall's course from Newcastle to Carlisle, coining the word 'milecastle' (Birley 1961, 14). The antiquary and cartographer John Warburton, who

FIGURE 46 Woodcut of William Camden. (Museum of Antiquities, University of Newcastle upon Tyne)

WILLIAM CAMBDEN Clarenciaux king of Armes. He dyed at Westminster Anno Dm 1623. Aged 74 yeares.

of time and resources limited him to the east, west and south gates and parts of the interior. However, it was not only his excavations at Housesteads and the discovery of Hadrianic building stones along the Wall that led him to this conclusion: he also appreciated that the siting of the forts, and the relation to them and to each other of the Wall and the Vallum, indicated unity of design and 'a fitness for the general purposes for which it was intended' (Birley 1961, 60). Hodgson's work without doubt set the agenda for future archaeological research along the middle lengths of Hadrian's Wall.

Clayton's excavations

John Clayton's archaeological career began in 1843 when he started excavating the Roman Fort of Cilurnum at his residence at Chesters. Under the supervision of his site director William Tailforth, a series of chambers near the east rampart was excavated and the work of clearing out other portions of the fort was continued (Budge 1903, 9). The *praetorium*, or Commandant's House, and the bath-house were also excavated in this year. In 1848 Clayton began excavating Milecastle 42 on his newly acquired land at Cawfields, explaining that there was 'more left of this Mile Castle than any other on the line of the Wall' (Clayton 1855a, 56). Clayton's excavations at Cawfields revealed much, including a building stone of the Twentieth Legion, known to have been in Britain during the reign of Hadrian. This added weight to John Hodgson's convictions that the Wall was originally built by Hadrian and not by Severus, as was still generally believed at the time. Clayton continued his excavations at Milecastle 37, west of Housesteads, in 1853 (Clayton 1855b, 269). The milecastle was cleared to establish its plan and revealed the considerable remains of the north gateway, complete with massive voussoirs found lying in the debris. It was also revealed that at one time 'during the latter part of the period of the occupation of Britain by the Romans, when their garrison grew feebler', the northern gateway had been narrowed (Clayton 1855a, 276). Another inscription referring to the governor Aulus Platorius Nepos was unearthed, making it the fourth stone bearing his name found in the milecastles in the vicinity of Housesteads. Work continued at Castle Nick, Milecastle 39, the following year, clearing the Roman walls and the interior, but not totally excavating the site. All three milecastles were cleared out and restored by Clayton for presentation, the walls built in an inferior manner to the Wall using loose stone cleared from the site and rebuilt on the surviving courses of Roman masonry without the use of mortar. The Roman walls were finally topped with a turf cap.

In 1852 Clayton turned his attention to Housesteads after a visit to the site of the First Pilgrimage to Hadrian's Wall by the Newcastle Society of Antiquaries in 1849. Clayton's major concern during his excavations was to expose the Roman walls of the fort to public view. Excavation of the gates, much of the curtain, the east wing of the *praetorium* and perhaps the outline of an interior building took place

(Bosanquet 1904, 201–3, 209). It was claimed by George Budge, curator of Chesters Museum, that by 1866 much of the interior had been exposed, but this may be an exaggeration (Budge 1903, 189). Damage to the walls and interior caused by the increasing number of tourists forced Clayton to infill the site to protect the remains, unfortunately before a complete plan of the excavations could be made (Budge 1903, 189). MacLauchlan's plan of 1850 shows the outline clearly but only the granaries are shown within the interior. The 1st Edition Ordnance Survey map of 1866 (sheet LXXXIII) similarly shows the walls and the granaries and also a bath-house by the north gateway and buildings by the south and east gateways. The bastle house by the south gateway is also exposed but most of the site appears not to have been dug or even surveyed. Certainly Bosanquet's workmen in 1898 encountered earlier digging and he reports them as saying 'That's no dout ald Antony's been here before us', a reference to Clayton's foreman, Anthony Place (Bosanquet 1904, 231). Although the extent of Clayton's excavations at Housesteads remains unclear, his work provided the first complete outline of a Roman fort known anywhere in Europe, and the first unequivocal evidence that Hadrian was the builder of the Roman Wall.

The 'Clayton Wall'

Possibly one of Clayton's most enduring works was the clearing and restoration of sections of the Wall itself. Sections of what is today known as the 'Clayton Wall' can be seen running through the estate on Peel Crags, Hotbank Crags and Housesteads Crags and remain a legacy to his dedication to the preservation of the Roman Wall. Clayton set his workmen to clear the Wall of its accumulated debris, exposing the core and surviving masonry, and rebuild it using the material removed from it. Facing-stones were relaid dry in level courses on the surviving Wall without the use of mortar or cement. New core was built up using some of the rubble left from the clearance and the top was capped with turf, taken from the adjacent grassland. The rebuilding was so successful that it is often difficult to distinguish the restoration from the original. The easiest way to define surviving Roman layers is to look for hard grey mortar between the stones. Where no mortar can be seen, grass growing up between the stones can often be an indication of original masonry, as can the presence of springwort, a lime-loving plant (Hodgson, 1822). Original Roman masonry is known to survive up to six or seven courses high at various points along the Wall, but in places is only two, or none at all.

Despite his dedication to the preservation of the Roman monuments, Clayton was not renowned for his record-keeping, and the exact date of his restoration of the Wall is unknown. However, it is most likely to date between 1848 and 1873, years which saw the most active archaeological investigation on the Chesters estate. The work was carried out by estate workmen, experienced in drystone walling but unsupervised by Clayton or an archaeologist. Inscribed stones found whilst clearing the Wall were kept but were often simply recorded as being found 'between Housesteads and Cawfields' (Collingwood and Wright 1965, 518). In a letter addressed to the Society of Antiquaries of Newcastle dated 1848, but not published in *Archaeologia Aeliana* until 1855, Clayton describes how 'the process of clearing away the debris of the Roman Wall on top of the Cawfields or Caw Gap Crags' had revealed 'a mural tablet ... in the face of the Wall'. He closes the letter with the promise that 'I will take care that the ruins of the ... Murus on the Cawfield Crags shall be carefully preserved in their present state.' An editor's postscript notes that by 1855 Cawfields Milecastle had been 'disinterred' but does not mention the Wall on the crags (Clayton 1855a, 58). However, by the time of the Second Pilgrimage along Hadrian's Wall in 1887 the work was probably complete, as 'John Clayton's ... loving restoration of long stretches of the Wall itself provided more and more for the visitor to see' (Birley 1961, 28).

Clayton's restoration of the Wall proved to be relatively successful, especially on level ground such as along Housesteads Crags. Other lengths, particularly parts on Hotbank Crags, present a less impressive monument, with irregular facing and unstable core (Crow 1995). Pedestrian and cattle damage causes wear to the upper courses of the Wall, and rain and frost erode the surviving Roman mortar, leading to bulging and occasionally collapse. However, despite the careful maintenance and frequent repair work required to sustain the Clayton Wall, the benefits of retaining it outweigh those of consolidating it using modern techniques. The Clayton method allows the surviving Roman core to 'breathe', thus preserving it, whereas consolidating the Wall using modern cement mortars causes the core to break down, therefore effectively removing the very thing that was meant to be preserved in the first place. The Clayton Wall is a shell designed to protect the surviving Roman remains and, despite recent attempts to find a mortar sympathetic to the survival of the core, it remains the best method of conservation. Simpson's repairs proved that with careful management and sympathetic restoration, the Clayton Wall can be maintained to a high standard. The National Trust is committed to continuing this tradition and to achieving sustainable high standards in the conservation of the Wall.

Dr John Collingwood Bruce

Clayton's interest in the Wall was equally matched by that of Dr John Collingwood Bruce (Figure 50) who, in 1848, unable to visit Europe due to 'revolutionary convulsions', 'went to the Roman Wall instead. I took with me my son Gainsford, then a lad of 14, and two artists, Mr Henry and Mr Charles Richardson. For our mutual convenience we had an open carriage with us, and my son had his pony. We did the wall pretty thoroughly, and brought away with us copious notes of the structure' (Bruce 1867, 135). The watercolours made by the Richardson brothers are of particular importance; not only do they show the condition of the surviving standing Wall before Clayton began his reconstruction, but they depict the existing farmhouses on the line of the Wall as well. The farmsteads at Shield-on-the-Wall, Caw Gap and Steel Rigg are clearly shown, as is the farmhouse at Housesteads. The watercolours are now held by the Laing Gallery in Newcastle (see plate 3).

Bruce became one of the leading exponents of the Wall. It has been said that as 'Clayton dug, Bruce wrote', and there can be no doubt that the work of each complemented the other's. Clayton's discoveries at Milecastle 42 led Bruce to champion the case that Hadrian was the original builder of the Roman Wall, and not Severus, a view still upheld by most Wall scholars. In 1851 Bruce published the first edition of *The Roman Wall*, which received over 300 subscriptions, including those of the Duke of Northumberland and the Lord Bishop of Durham. The

Figure 50
Dr John Collingwood Bruce, populist and self-publicist, in typical pose, *c*.1870. (Museum of Antiquities, University of Newcastle upon Tyne)

F. G. Simpson (1882–1955)

Little work was carried out along the rest of the Wall in the middle section during this period until Frank Gerald Simpson began excavations with J. P. Gibson at the fort on the Stanegate at Haltwhistle Burn in 1907 (Figure 53). Excavations over two seasons revealed both the south and east gates and the whole of the inner face of the north rampart was cleared, proving that no gate had existed on that side (Gibson & Simpson 1909, 9). The slight remains of five interior buildings were found, one of which may have been the *praetorium* (Site VI). The site, however, was noted for its paucity of pottery finds which, with other evidence from within the buildings, suggested that it was abandoned and deliberately dismantled. Simpson and Gibson concluded that the fort was built to protect the Stanegate where it crossed the deep valley of the burn (Simpson traced the Stanegate's route in 1908), and went out of use after the building of the Wall in the AD 130s. In the years 1907–8 Simpson also excavated a Roman watermill on the east bank of the Haltwhistle Burn and a possibly medieval building on Burnhead Crags, now destroyed by quarrying (Simpson, G. 1976, 77–80). In 1908, too, trenches were dug through the Vallum at Cawfields to investigate its construction, and the Military Way was traced for 24.1 km (15 miles) to the east of the Haltwhistle Burn (Simpson, G. 1976, 116).

FIGURE 53 F. G. Simpson (1882–1955). (Museum of Antiquities, University of Newcastle upon Tyne)

In 1909 work began to restore the line of Hadrian's Wall on Peel Crags. It had fallen into a state of such disrepair that the Chesters estate originally intended to remove it and replace it with a drystone wall. The restoration of the Clayton Wall formed a great deal of Simpson's work, and he was able to devise a method of repairing the damage as well as ensuring the survival of the existing Roman material. His method, published by his daughter Grace in *Watermills and Military Works on Hadrian's Wall* (1976), is still applied by the National Trust in their annual repairs to the fabric of the Clayton Wall. In 1911 Simpson wrote:

> Damage by pedestrians and cattle is generally confined to the upper courses, and may be made good simply by the replacement of the fallen stones with the addition of fresh turf. The damage due to frost and beating rain is much more serious. It is especially so in the case of the Wall, on account of the wide joints between the facing-stones and the condition of the mortar. The latter, though extremely hard and well preserved at certain points, it is for the most parts soft, and in many cases entirely decayed. As a result of exposure of the Wall from about the year 1848, the mortar was soon washed out of the joints, from the face inwards, causing the heavy, wedge shaped stones to slide downward and forward, thus affecting not only the top courses, but, frequently, the full height of the exposed face, which bulges and finally collapses, carrying away the whole face at that point.

As a means of preventing the bulging, Simpson argued that cement grouting behind the face would not be satisfactory, because it could not prevent the further erosion of the old mortar from the joints. He was doubtful whether an existing bulge could be rectified any other way than by the removal of the old mortar. This of course necessitates the temporary removal of the facing-stones, which may be replaced with new mortar kept back from the face of the joints, or dry-built. In the present case, the heavy cost of cement, or mortar, made its use impracticable, except at points specially liable to damage such as the corners of gateways, and the work was therefore dry-built, much as Clayton had done some sixty years earlier:

> The facing-stones were on no account dressed, or altered, to suit a particular position, or depth of course. In the absence of any jointing material, the courses were laid directly one upon another, the spaces between the inner, roughly pointed, ends of the facing-stones, formerly occupied by mortar, being tightly packed with fallen stone from the core, broken small. Finally the top of the repaired portion was covered in turf. The size and weight of the facing-stones, together with the friction of the packing, appears to ensure a very stable structure, judging from the state of the repairs after five or six years.

Doubts were raised at the time whether or not after a few years it would be possible to distinguish between the original Roman material and the later restoration. Simpson was convinced that there was a marked difference between the original core and the stone packing behind the repaired face. While the core was composed for the most part of pieces of basalt as large as facing stones, the stones of the modern packing used were generally about the size of road-metal. Later recording has shown that although narrow joints and the absence of mortar does not necessarily denote repair-work, the evidence of stone packing is usually decisive.

than anticipated and a complex structural sequence against the north curtain wall. Detailed recording of the surviving stonework of the bastle and south gate was under taken by Alan Whitworth in advance of consolidation in 1986 (Whitworth 1990).

Recent excavations and surveys

Between 1982 and 1988 excavations along the line of the Wall were undertaken by the National Trust with generous assistance from English Heritage under the direction of James Crow. The excavations were carried out because of the severe erosion to the footpath in the steep-sided gaps of the Whin Sill, especially between Highshield Crags and Peel Crags, and at Peel Gap, that had occurred as a result of an increase in visitor numbers. Altogether about 400 m of the Wall were excavated together with the interior of Milecastle 39, the north gate of Milecastle 37 and the tower in Peel Gap (Crow 1989, 53). Excavations between 1986 and 1988 along the Wall in Peel Gap revealed a sequence of building periods consisting of a broad foundation, Hadrianic Narrow Wall and extra-narrow Severan rebuild on top of that. On the south face of the Wall there was an unexpected find of an additional tower in the turret system along Wall Mile 39 (see pp. 40–42). The discovery of a whitewashed chamfered stone in the north face suggested that the Wall may originally have been whitened. Excavations along the Wall in the Castle Nick/Highshield Crags area revealed an isolated section of Broad Wall foundation on Mons Fabricius that had been ignored by the later rebuilders and had been cleared away before rebuilding on the steep slope running up to Highshield Crag (Figure 54).

During excavations samples of Roman mortar were removed to be analysed by the Building Research Establishment, who were looking for suitable ancient mortars to serve as 'natural analogues to modern concrete' (Crow 1989, 45). Findings suggested the locations of some of the limestone quarries used by the Severan rebuilders and it seems that local limestone outcrops were not exploited. A Roman limekiln is known at Housesteads and there is another possible one on Queen's Crags, lying just to the north of the Trust estate. Research to find a suitable modern mortar that does not erode the original Roman mortar is continuing on the Wall on Highshield Crag (Teutonico *et al.* 1993, 34).

At Milecastle 37 the north wall and gate were investigated before consolidation of the south side and three phases of building were found (Daniels 1989, 55). Milecastle 39 was excavated between 1985 and 1987 revealing the interior buildings (Daniels 1989, 53). On Mons Fabricius a group of shielings with pottery dating from the early fourteenth century up to possibly the early sixteenth was excavated and consolidated for display (Crow 1995) and a native settlement north of Bradley farmhouse was discovered and surveyed (Daniels 1989, 53). No systematic excavations have been conducted on the estate since 1989 and work carried out on the Wall has

FIGURE 54 Diggers excavating the site of three medieval shielings alongside Hadrian's Wall on Mons Fabricius, 1987. The foundations of the Broad Wall can be seen in the foreground. The last great phase of excavations along the Wall was carried out by the National Trust (with funding from English Heritage) between 1982 and 1989. (Photo: J. Crow, 1987)

been limited to the maintenance of the Clayton Wall. Between 1983 and 1989 the 'old' estate from Housesteads to East Bog was surveyed by the National Trust at a scale of 1:1000. The north-east corner of the estate was not included as it was considered to be too archaeologically sparse (although it was briefly surveyed in 1987 by David Cowley and archaeology students from the University of Newcastle upon Tyne) and neither were Cawfields and Shield-on-the-Wall farms, as they lay outside the National Trust estate at the time of the survey. However, the archaeological remains within the boundaries of the farms have now been recorded in part by the Royal Commission on the Historical Monuments of England (RCHME) in its Linear Survey of Hadrian's Wall and the Cawfields Camp survey (see below). An assessment of the current state of the archaeological remains on Cawfields Farm was carried out by Clare White on its acquisition by the National Trust in 1992.

Between 1986 and 1991 the entire length of Hadrian's Wall was recorded by the RCHME at a scale of 1:2500. The Hadrian's Wall Linear Survey was predominantly concerned with recording the Wall, the Vallum, Military Way and Wall-ditch and any features that may impinge upon the Wall or any of the other linear features. The Wall survey was complemented by an earlier survey of the Roman temporary camps surrounding the Haltwhistle Burn on Cawfields Farm at a scale of 1:1000. Haltwhistle Burn fortlet was excluded from the survey but temporary camps Haltwhistle Burn 1, Haltwhistle Burn 2 and 3, Markham Cottage 1 and 2, Cawfields, Haltwhistle Burn 4 and Milestone House were surveyed and accompanied with text (Welfare and Swan, 1995). The Stanegate where it passes through Cawfields Camp was similarly surveyed at this time at a scale of 1:1000. In 1986 the RCHME completed a survey of Housesteads Fort, *vicus* and surrounding area at a scale of 1:1000, recording features of all periods in remarkable detail. The surveys carried out by the National Trust and the RCHME in the 1980s provide an extraordinary record of a unique landscape in the British Isles.

In 1997, following the completion of this study, the National Trust acquired 48.6 ha (120 acres) of land north of Broomlee Lough. The Trust intends to carry out a systematic archaeological survey here to increase our understanding and complete the recording of this remarkable landscape. Most recently, in 1998 the Archaeological Practice of the University of Newcastle upon Tyne undertook an evaluation of the remains of a shieling in the Bogle Hole. Despite almost 300 years of research along the Wall, the prehistoric, Roman, medieval and post-medieval occupation of this corner of Northumberland will undoubtedly continue to attract archaeologists well into the twenty-first century.

8
A NORTHUMBERLAND LANDSCAPE FROM PREHISTORY TO THE PRESENT DAY

The National Trust Hadrian's Wall estate contains possibly one of the densest concentrations of archaeological sites in the north of England (Figure 55). Despite the fact that settlement was often short-lived, and at times only seasonal, there can be no doubt that human activity has had a tremendous impact on the making of the landscape as we know it today. Yet in the shadow of the Whin Sill, much of this activity may seem somewhat superficial; after all, the nature of human settlement on the estate is partly due to the marginal nature of the land. High above the Tyne valley, on the edge of the great wastes of Northumberland, the occupation of this landscape must have seemed less than favourable. The view north of the Wall undoubtedly is often bleak and forbidding, and the weather can be dreadful, even in summer. The wind is relentless all year round, bringing a chill even on the sunniest of days. Every visitor to Housesteads feels pity for the countless legionaries who shivered in this northernmost part of the Empire. They, of course,

FIGURE 55 The Housesteads palimpsest, 1907. Overlying the Roman fort and *vicus* are the remains of medieval and post-medieval farmsteads. The current farmhouse was built by John Clayton in *c.*1860. (J. P. Gibson)

FIGURE 56 Building inscription of the Second Legion dated to the second century AD, one of the key pieces of evidence for attributing the building of the Wall to Hadrian and not his successors. (Museum of Antiquities, University of Newcastle upon Tyne)

would have had little choice over where they were posted, but, as the archaeological record demonstrates, others made the conscious decision to settle here for thousands of years.

Although there are only a few known prehistoric sites on the estate, their importance to our understanding of the landscape cannot be ignored. To understand them fully, they must be studied in the context of the wider landscape of the upland areas of the South Tyne valley and beyond. More and more information is being gathered by the Tyne-Solway Landscape Project based at the Department of Archaeology in the University of Newcastle upon Tyne. The palaeobotanical evidence recovered from Crag Lough by students from the University of Newcastle upon Tyne in 1992 has provided a fascinating insight into the early prehistoric environment and the effects of human activity upon it. Evidence for woodland clearance and an increase in grassland and plantain species both indicate that pastoralism was carried out in the Bronze Age. The increase in the levels of cereal pollen at this time also suggests a growth in upland populations. Extensive cultivation, coupled with a deterioration in climate, led to the loss of tree cover and the establishment of peat in some areas. In this upland region woodland, once cleared, was unable to regenerate, and survived only in more sheltered locations. However, the nature of the native population before the arrival of the Romans remains shadowy and the lack of any definite occupation site on the estate makes comment on prehistoric settlement difficult. Further research into this period is needed, but over a wider area, so as to help us to understand the early occupation of this landscape.

Roman activity in this part of Northumberland has been the subject of research for almost 300 years, ever since Christopher Hunter visited Housesteads in 1702. Despite the large number of excavations and surveys carried out this century, it is highly likely that the Wall will continue to attract interest from scholars and visitors alike well into the next millennium. There are, after all, a great number of questions still to be answered: most importantly, why was the Wall actually built? and why did it remain in use for so long? Numerous theories about the reasons for its construction have been suggested over the years: it was built 'to keep the Picts out', to 'control communications between North and South', to 'divide the trouble-some Brigantes tribe', or even simply to 'occupy the Roman army to stop them revolting'. The truth is that we still do not fully understand exactly why it was built and, sadly, nor are we ever likely to. It is the nature of archaeology, however, both to continue to ask more questions and to find new angles of research, which will bring us closer to a broader understanding of the origins of the Wall (Figure 56).

One of the most remarkable aspects of Hadrian's Wall is that it was continually occupied for almost 300 years. It is hard to know if Hadrian ever envisaged his wall to have been a permanent feature, although it is unlikely that so much time and money would have been invested into it if he had not. It has been suggested that the Wall was built by Hadrian simply as a means of keeping his potentially rebellious troops occupied. Eighteenth-century landowners would often employ local out-of-work labourers to build follies or eye-catchers in their parks and gardens, not only out of a sense of munificence, but to ensure that, whilst occupied, they would not turn to crime or, worse still, turn against the landowner himself. Hadrian's Wall, however, was no folly; although it may have been safer to maintain a large army a long distance from Rome, there can be no doubt that the Wall had a serious role to play in the overseeing of the north of Britain.

The advance northwards by Hadrian's successor, Antoninus Pius, shows that, as the other frontiers, or *limes*, of the Roman Empire were in a constant state of flux, so was the northern frontier. The return to the line of the Wall following the abandonment of the Antonine Wall in the AD 160s indicates not a failure on Pius's part, but that the original frontier provided the best location for the Roman centre of command for the north of Britain. The rebuilding work by the emperor Severus in the early third century underlines this. It has been suggested that the intention of Severus's campaigns in Scotland was not to subjugate and exploit the landscape, but to systematically devastate it by burning crops and killing off livestock, and so leaving the population to starve, ensuring a peace that lasted for a further 100 years. With this in mind, it is not unreasonable to suggest that following Severus's death, the role of the Wall changed. From functioning simply as a base for expeditions north, it became a fixed and permanent frontier (in the modern sense of the word), beyond which lay an enfeebled population who could pose no threat to the south.

such as the Hadrian's Wall estate, but less is known of domestic occupation and agricultural practice. The farmstead at Steel Rigg is but one example of a type of settlement found throughout the uplands of Northumberland, but about which surprisingly little is known. Small farms and holdings played as much of a role in the shaping of the landscape as the large landowners, but their contribution is perhaps less understood. The key to making sense of the post-medieval landscape is the combining of historical and archaeological research. Social history also has a vital role to play and can help piece together the lives of those who lived along the line of the Wall over the last few hundred years (Figure 57)

It seems that, following the decline of the Roman Empire, Hadrian's Wall had little influence over later settlement in this part of Northumberland. Settlement from the Middle Ages was determined not by the line of the Wall but by climatic, economic and political factors. The line of the Whin Sill and the marginal nature of the land, coupled with the instability brought about by the warring Border families, led to only small-scale occupation until the eighteenth century. Even then, the Roman Wall was generally considered an irrelevance, good only as a quarry for building stone or as bedding for the Military Way between Newcastle and Carlisle. Later, as a result of the Enclosure Acts of the 1790s, drystone walls were laid straight through the Roman remains with little consideration for the latter's survival. Not until the nineteenth century, when antiquaries began to take an interest in the actual physical remains of the Wall, did it reclaim its importance in the Northumberland landscape.

From country estate to World Heritage Site

When Hadrian's Wall was designated a World Heritage Site by UNESCO in 1987, this was seen as the first step in bringing together the vast numbers of disparate groups who live and work along the Wall to create a strategy for its management. In June 1996 English Heritage published its Hadrian's Wall Management Plan outlining proposals for the protection of the Wall over the next 30 years. But, as this study has shown, Hadrian's Wall has been intensely managed since the mid-nineteenth century, when it was the centre of the Clayton estate. Both the landscape and the structural archaeology as we know it today owes as much to the work of John Clayton as to Hadrian and his successors.

Hadrian's Wall had been attracting the attention of scholars since the sixteenth century, with the publication by William Camden of his influential *Britannia* in 1586. It was not until 1702, however, that Christopher Hunter took his life in his hands and became the first antiquary to visit Housesteads. The early eighteenth century saw a number of authorial publications on Roman Britain, most notably Horsley's *Britannia Romana* in 1732, as well as an enormous growth in interest in classical antiquities. It became a part of every young gentleman's education to view the ruins of Europe whilst on the Grand Tour, Rome being popular with most. Many of the

FIGURE 57 A family group in front of Crag End farmstead *c*.1900, possibly relatives of the last occupants of this remote and ancient croft. (Northumberland National Park)

more portable objects were taken back to England in order to embellish the libraries and drawing-rooms of country houses, as well as to enrich the growing number of museums.

The antiquities of Britain attracted a more staunch and perhaps less well-positioned member of English society. Although unquestionably gentlemen, men such as William Hutton, the Rev. John Skinner and Dr John Lingard, who each walked the length of Hadrian's Wall at the turn of the nineteenth century, did not have the expense of visiting Italy. Dr John Collingwood Bruce, although from a wealthy family, was prevented from undertaking the Grand Tour by the continuing wars in Europe, and so instead became an authority on the Wall. These men typified the rise of the middle classes in early nineteenth-century Britain: reasonably well-off but not landed, they had the time to indulge their interest in the past.

It was from such a background that John Clayton came. Both he and his father had made their money from investment and development rather than land, which perhaps made his acquisition of much of the length of Hadrian's Wall all the more unusual. Clayton's alarm at the gradual quarrying of the Wall for stone to use in the building of new farmhouses and cottages led him to buy up land along its length to ensure its protection. This was probably one of the first acts of deliberate archaeological conservation in the world and brought about what can best be described as an 'archaeological park'. Clayton's contemporary, General Pitt Rivers, had created a similar arrangement on his land at Cranborne Chase in Dorset, which he opened

FIGURE 58 Men of the Wall. Clayton's and Bosanquet's workforces were made up of local farmers and labourers who knew the land well. Excavation provided vital extra income for the surrounding communities and most digging work was carried out in winter during the quiet months of the agricultural year. (Museum of Antiquities, University of Newcastle upon Tyne)

to the public to allow them to view the remains of the 'Ancient Britons'. The difference was that Pitt Rivers had inherited his estates, whilst Clayton was willing to invest his personal fortune in acquiring land solely for the protection of the Roman remains. The Clayton estate, therefore, was unlike any other, and it was not until the founding of the National Trust in 1895 that land was again bought up solely in the interests of conservation.

Clayton's influence on the management of the landscape was enormous. Having ensured the protection of the Wall, the estate was run on a commercial basis, effectively repaying the cost of the initial investment. Farmhouses were removed from the line of the Wall and rebuilt to the highest quality elsewhere. Cultivation was finally abandoned in favour of pasture, and better strains of livestock were introduced. Trees were planted not only as windbreaks around the farms, but also for commercial enterprise. Industry was permitted on a small scale to meet the needs of the local population, but the ironstone quarry on Cawfields Common may well have been closed by Clayton in about 1860 in order to ensure the protection of the Roman remains. The excavation of the Roman forts and milecastles, as well as the founding of the Clayton Wall, also provided additional seasonal employment for local farmers and labourers, many of whom became quite expert in the disinterment of ancient remains (Figure 58)

Above all, ownership gave Clayton the ability to carry out restoration work to the line of the Wall itself, as well as to excavate Cawfields and Housesteads. The protection the estate gave to not only Hadrian's Wall, but also its landscape, cannot be doubted. Almost as soon as the estate was broken up at the turn of the twentieth century, quarrying began at Cawfields, destroying about 50 m of the Wall. More quarrying took place at Shield-on-the-Wall, and in 1930 came the announcement of plans to extract whinstone from almost the entire length of the Whin Sill as far as Housesteads, leaving just the line of the Wall balancing on a paper-thin wedge of stone. Only a public outcry prevented its destruction.

Clayton's restoration of the Wall in many respects set a precedent for future conservation. He realised that the only way in which to ensure the protection of the Wall and its setting was through direct ownership and control. In establishing his estate, however, he brought about the predominance of one period of history, the Roman, over all others, a view that perhaps continues to this day. Clayton, along with many of his contemporaries, regarded later features, such as medieval settlements and eighteenth-century farmhouses, as an encumbrance upon the superior remains of the Roman Wall. The concept of 'Hadrian's Wall and its Setting' is, therefore, very much a Victorian idea, as much of the 'setting' as we know it today is the result of nineteenth-century landscaping carried out in order to protect the Wall. However, the remains of the prehistoric, medieval and post-medieval sites should not be considered merely an afterthought, since it can perhaps be argued that they form a more important element of the landscape than the Wall itself. Hadrian's Wall is, after all, a unique feature in the British Isles. Until the mid-nineteenth century, the formation of this Northumberland landscape perhaps owed more to the generations of settlers and farmers who have lived here since the second millennium BC than to the building of the Roman Wall. Nevertheless, Hadrian's Wall remains central to the landscape. Without it there would perhaps be no estate or World Heritage Site, and the Whin Sill may easily have been lost to quarrying. Unlike so much of the archaeology on the estate, the Wall is a tangible object that can be seen and touched, and there is no doubt that it will continue to be the main attraction for visitors. It is hoped that a greater understanding of the historic landscape will ensure future protection for more than just the Wall and its associated features. The National Trust estate forms only a tiny fragment of the Northumberland landscape, and yet within it lies an enormous number of sites of archaeological and historical interest. This pattern is repeated along almost the entire length of the Wall, from Wallsend to Bowness, which has implications not only for our interpretation but also for the protection and conservation of the whole landscape.

It is hoped that this publication has highlighted the truly historic nature of the

Deserted medieval village (DMV)

Term used by archaeologists to describe the remains of a settlement occupied during the medieval period but subsequently abandoned. Bradley Green represents such a site.

Drove road

Unmetalled track along which livestock were driven from Scotland to the markets in the South. In use from the medieval period to the nineteenth century. Such a route passes through Busy Gap and past Steel Rigg.

Enclosure Act

During the period 1783–1844 Acts of Parliament were passed to *inclose* the upland areas of the country. In the area covered by the estate, enclosure was usually by drystone wall, although hedges were also used. The majority of field boundaries found on the estate date from this time. Land in South Tynedale was enclosed by township, the borders of which were roughly equivalent to those of the modern civil parish. Thorngrafton (now part of Bardon Mill civil parish), Henshaw and Melkridge were enclosed by Act of Parliament between 1783 and 1797 whilst Haltwhistle (essentially Cawfields Farm) was not enclosed until 1844. Ridley Common (the land now occupied by the eastern part of Hotbank Farm north of Hadrian's Wall, and again now part of Bardon Mill civil parish) was enclosed by Private Agreement in 1751. The Enclosure Acts probably represented the single most influential change in the landscape of the estate since the building of Hadrian's Wall almost 1,700 years earlier.

Extra-narrow wall

See under **Narrow Wall**

Farmstead

Group of features comprising farmhouse, farm buildings and associated enclosures in permanent occupation (Ramm *et al.* 1970, xiv, 44–6). In this study the term normally refers to late seventeenth- and early eighteenth-century settlements.

Hadrian's Wall

Built by the Roman emperor Hadrian between AD 122 and AD 130, the Wall formed the northern boundary of the Roman Empire until the turn of the fifth century AD, except for short periods when the Antonine Wall was occupied in Scotland (*c.*AD 143–60). The Wall ran from Wallsend in the east to Bowness-on-Solway in the west and in the middle lengths runs along the crags of the Whin Sill. The exact height of the Wall is uncertain, but it may possibly have been up to 4.5 m high. The section of Hadrian's Wall between Chesters Roman fort in Northumberland and Birdoswald fort in Cumbria is known as the middle lengths.

Hedge bank

Earthwork boundary on which hedges were planted in the early modern period both before and during the period of the Enclosure Acts (1783–1844). Relict, disused hedge banks are found throughout the Hadrian's Wall estate, most prominently at Steel Rigg, and reflect patterns of historic land use.

Limekiln

A structure intended for the burning of limestone to produce lime, used mostly for agricultural purposes. A limekiln consists of a large, stone-built bowl, about 3 m in internal diameter, parallel sided 2.5 m or so and then tapering downwards rapidly to the bottom. The whole was contained in a very sturdy enclosing structure, a massive tower, perhaps 2.5 m thick at the side of the bowl, circular or square in section. The top of the kiln was situated below the level of a quarry floor, so broken limestone could be tipped in. Draw arches at the front allowed the burnt lime and ashes to be drawn out. Examples on the estate can be found at Bradley Farm and north of Cuddy's Crags.

Marching camp

See under **Temporary camps**

Milecastle

A small walled fortlet incorporating barracks and gateways to north and south linked by a central

roadway, provided at approximate intervals of
1 Roman mile (1480 m) for the whole length of
Hadrian's Wall. Modern convention numbers these
from 1 (Wallsend) to 80 (Bowness, Cumbria).
Milecastles 37, 38, 39, 41 and 42 lie within the estate
boundaries.

Military Road (now the B6318)

Constructed by General Wade between 1751 and
1757 in response to the English army's failure to
cross the country to counter the Jacobite Rebellion
in 1745. For most of its length it lies upon the line of
Hadrian's Wall but in the area of the estate it spares
the Wall and follows the line of the Vallum between
Highshield Farm and Winshields.

Military Way

Roman road running parallel to and between
Hadrian's Wall and the Vallum providing access to
milecastles, turrets and forts. Built after the Wall
system was reoccupied after the abandonment of the
Antonine Wall in Scotland in the AD 160s.

Narrow Wall

Hadrian's Wall as completed and in parts rebuilt
and not finished to Broad Wall specification.
Narrow Wall signifies those portions finished to a
narrower gauge. 'Extra-narrow wall' is a term
often used to describe sections of Hadrian's Wall
rebuilt by the emperor Septimius Severus and his
successors.

Palaeobotanical evidence

Ancient botanical and environmental remains
that can identify natural and human-induced
vegetation changes. Ancient land use (such as
cereal cultivation or woodland clearance) not
otherwise visible in the archaeological record can
therefore be identified. Palaeobotanical samples
were taken from Crag Lough in 1992 and have
provided important evidence for the prehistory of
the estate.

Peel, or pele

Originally a fortified enclosure; by the late Middle
Ages the term had acquired a wide range of

meanings and was often used as a synonym for
tower or to describe almost any defensible
construction (Ramm *et al.* 1970, xiv, 61).

Ridge and furrow

The earthwork remains of medieval cultivation,
measuring up to 7 m between furrows with
characteristic 'inverted-S'-shaped ridges. Examples
are known at Bradley Green. Later post-medieval
ridge and furrow, practised in the upland areas of
South Tynedale until the early nineteenth century,
measures less than 5 m between furrows. Its ridges
are quite straight and often lie within Enclosure Act
boundaries, which suggests a date during the period
of the wars with France, 1793–1815.

Shieling

A small hut built during the medieval and post-
medieval periods. Made of unmortared rubble
and occasionally turf, they were used by
persons practising 'shielding', a dialect term for
transhumance, the practice of moving livestock to
upland pastures and living with them during the
summer months. Shieling grounds refer to the
upland area where shielings were to be found.
Examples of shielings are known throughout the
estate, most notably on Mons Fabricius and in
the Bogle Hole, and the name has been retained
in many places, such as Highshield and Shield-on-
the-Wall.

Stack stand

Early modern-period earthwork circular enclosure
with bank and ditch, constructed to form a fairly
level, dry platform on which to pile a stack of winter
fodder (Ramm *et al.* 1970, 54).

Standing stones

Upright stones placed into the ground, often found
in circles or groups of three or four, forming part
of the late Neolithic/early Bronze Age landscape,
with possible ritual or territorial connotations.
The Mare and Foal on Cawfields Farm are the
remains of a group of at least three, if not four,
standing stones.

Stanegate

The Roman road built in the late first century AD connecting the recently established forts at Corbridge and Carlisle. Haltwhistle Burn Fortlet was built on the line of the Stanegate at the turn of the second century AD. The Stanegate passes through the estate in Cawfields Farm.

Temporary camps

Roman camps with turf-built ramparts, often built as over-night accommodation by Roman troops on campaign or for use during the building of the Wall. Others may be 'practice' camps thrown up by the army on training manoeuvres. The camps at Cawfields are some of the best preserved along the length of the Wall. Haltwhistle Burn Fortlet is not a temporary camp and was permanently occupied until the building of the Wall (Welfare and Swan 1995).

Tramway

Raised earthwork bank with a levelled surface on which tracks and sleepers were laid. Trolleys were used on the tramways to carry ironstone, whinstone, coal, lime, etc. An important tramway ran from Cawfields Quarry down the Haltwhistle Burn to Haltwhistle. Also occasionally known as wagonways and tubways.

Turret

Small rectangular tower, spaced between milecastles at intervals of a third of a Roman mile. Incorporated into the fabric of the Wall but decommissioned by the early third century AD. Modern convention numbers these in sequence from the east end of the Wall 0a, 0b, 1a, 1b and so on, taking their numbers from the milecastle to the east. Turrets 37a, 37b, 38a, 38b, 39a, 39b, 40b, 41a and 41b lie within the estate, with an additional tower in the Wall system at Peel Gap.

Vallum

A flat-bottomed ditch flanked by mounds running to the south of Hadrian's Wall. It post-dates the building of the Wall but is part of the same system and may have been built to delimit a military zone, although there is no real evidence for this. It appears to have gone out of use by the end of the second century AD. The only known crossings are at forts such as Housesteads.

Vicus

The settlement, normally of civilians, clustered around the outside of Housesteads Fort, and others along the length of Hadrian's Wall. The consolidated buildings outside the south gate of Housesteads Fort are under the guardianship of English Heritage.

Voussoir

A wedge-shaped stone forming part of an arch.

Wall-ditch

V-shaped ditch running parallel to the north of Hadrian's Wall. Unlike the Vallum, the ditch is not continuous and was only cut at points where the Wall is not naturally defended by the crags, for example, Milking Gap, Rapishaw Gap.

Wall-mile

A wall-mile is defined by the distance between milecastles (see above)

GAZETTEER OF ARCHAEOLOGICAL FEATURES

In May 1994 an archaeological survey of the Hadrian's Wall estate was commissioned by the National Trust, the objectives of which were a) to compile a Sites and Monuments Record (SMR) or gazetteer of every archaeological feature on the estate, b) to provide a comprehensive history of the estate and the archaeological investigation that has been carried out on it since the time of the earliest antiquaries, and c) to provide recommendations for the management of the archaeology on the estate. Hadrian's Wall, especially those parts restored by Clayton in the nineteenth century, is particularly vulnerable to pressure caused by visitors walking along its top. This leads to erosion of the surface, which can cause the faces of the Wall to bulge and occasionally collapse. It was important, therefore, for the survey to identify areas of erosion and potential damage so that repairs to the Wall could be made before further damage occurred. The condition and vulnerability of all the archaeological sites found on the estate were similarly assessed. The survey also included drystone walls and other field boundaries, such as fences and relict hedge-bank boundaries.

The National Trust Sites and Monuments Record

Since 1994 the National Trust has maintained its own computerised Sites and Monuments Record database. The survey of the Hadrian's Wall estate was the first place in the country where the new database was put to active use.

The nature of the archaeology on the estate provided a test of the SMR's flexibility; Hadrian's Wall runs for about 10km (6 miles) through the estate and differs immensely in condition from nineteenth-century restoration and twentieth-century consolidation to unexcavated lengths buried underneath drystone walls. The main difficulty was how to enter this notoriously awkward linear feature, which snakes its way over the crags and gaps of the Whin Sill, changing in form at irregular intervals, into the records structure provided by the SMR. The problem was solved by dividing the Wall up into clearly identifiable lengths defined by modern field boundaries or by changes in the form of the Wall. The Vallum, Wall-ditch and Military Way presented a similar problem and it was again decided to break these features down into shorter, more manageable sections, as defined by Ordnance Survey (OS) field parcels and tenancy boundaries. Other sites were more straightforward and could be given individual site descriptions. In all, 516 records were entered into the SMR.

Public access to the National Trust's SMR is available by contacting the Head of Archaeology, The National Trust Estates Advisory Office, 33 Sheep Street, Cirencester, Gloucestershire GL7 1RQ.

Selective list of sites

For the purposes of this publication, the SMR has been adapted to produce a simplified gazetteer of the archaeological features, highlighting not only their importance, but also the enormous diversity of the surviving archaeological record found on the National Trust's Hadrian's Wall estate (Figure 60). The SMR now plays an important role in the management of this extraordinary historic landscape, helping the Trust to balance the needs of conservation with those of modern agriculture and public access.

For architectural terms the reader is referred to

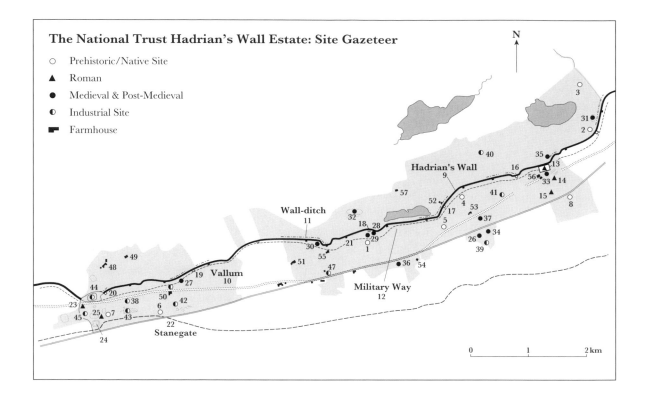

FIGURE 60 Map showing the key archaeological sites on the National Trust Hadrian's Wall estate. (R. Woodside)

John Fleming, Hugh Honour and Nikolaus Pevsner, *The Penguin Dictionary of Architecture* (4th edn, London 1981) and Jean-Pierre Adam, *Roman Building: Materials and Techniques* (London 1994) for further information.

Prehistoric sites

Site 1 Bronze Age boundary wall

OS Grid Ref NY 75616737 – NY 76216771

The boundary consists of large whinstone boulders in a line on the east side of Sycamore Gap. It is cut by the Military Way and then can be traced for about 20 m running into the mire south of Peel Crags. In 1983 Judy Turner of Durham University observed palaeo-environmental

evidence dating back to the Bronze Age deposited on the boulder wall in the mire. The wall re-emerges from the mire heading west by the modern farm track to Sycamore Gap, and runs discontinuously alongside the track in OS Field Parcel 6345. The line of the wall is less distinct along this length. The purpose of the wall is unknown, but seems to mark the division between the mire and the crags.

Site 2 King's Crags prehistoric boundary

OS Grid Ref NY 79746937

Boundary feature consisting of turf and stone up to 1 m wide. It forms a distinct lip away from the base of the crags and so is not simply fallen crag material. Furthermore, it is truncated by the Wall-ditch in Busy Gap and so without doubt is prehistoric. The presence of a similar boundary in Sycamore Gap and the mire south of Peel Crags suggests that it, too, may be Bronze Age in date. The purpose of the boundary is not known, but it has been suggested that it acted as a symbolic demarcation of territory reconfirming earlier divisions previously defined by the Whin Sill.

Site 3 Black Dyke linear earthwork
OS Grid Ref NY 79956992 – NY 79527059

The Black Dyke is a linear earthwork running between the South Tyne at Haydon Bridge and the North Tyne at Carriteth Cottage (Spain 1921, 121–68). Pre-Roman earthwork with bank and ditch. The ditch is always on the west, up to 1.8 m deep. Its purpose is unknown. The line of the dyke is often lost as it passes through boggy mosses, re-emerging on the drier land on the other side. The general line is north–south with a convex curve to the west. Only the better sections are discernible. In the estate, the line of the dyke can be seen running from the bottom of Sewingshields Crags to Queen's Crags, surviving up to 1.4 m high and up to 4 m wide. The ditch is up to 0.4 m deep and 1.6 m wide. The dyke survives only intermittently along this stretch and is surmounted by a mid-eighteenth-century drystone wall.

Site 4 Bradley Farm native settlement
OS Grid Ref NY 777596818

Rectilinear native settlement with 4 hut circles measuring 4.7 to 5.3 m internally, with stone-faced walls up to 0.5 m wide and up to 0.4 m high. The enclosure wall is made of single boulders 0.4 m high and there are traces of 2 internal walls. The settlement is located close to a stream. Its exact date is unknown, but it appears similar in form to that at Milking Gap, not far to the south-west. The size of the hut circles and the nature of the ring-walls suggest a Romano-British date rather than Bronze Age (Burgess 1984, 146).

Site 5 Milking Gap native settlement
OS Grid Ref NY 77246779

The settlement at Milking Gap, excavated by Kilbride-Jones in 1937, consists of a rectangular enclosure containing 3 hut circles and interior dividing walls and 2 further hut circles outside the enclosure walls. At a distance from the enclosure of 4.8 m to the north-east is a small cairn, 5.45 m in diameter. The enclosure walls are made up of double-face boulders up to 0.8 m high and 2 m wide, with an entrance on the east side. The enclosure is centred around a hut circle, 7 m in diameter, from which radiate 4 dividing walls, each with entrances. There are 2 further, less well-preserved hut circles within the enclosure and 2 more outside to the south. There are 2 more possible hut circles to the south-east. Possibly associated are 3 relict boulder walls running out from the settlement. Pottery finds have provided a date of between AD 122 and 180. It has been suggested that the settlement was forced out of use by the Romans at the time of the building of the Vallum. However, there is no real evidence of this and a re-assessment of the evidence is required.

Site 6 Mare and Foal standing stones
OS Grid Ref NY 72546632

Located just N of the Stanegate, 2 standing stones, the north stone standing 1.51 m high, the south 0.98 m at a distance apart of 4.82 m. The 1769 Armstrong map of Northumberland marks 3 stones *in situ*. It has been suggested that the stones formed part of a larger feature known as a 'four-poster', ie 4 monoliths arranged in a square. Loose boulders were packed around the base of the stones to prevent damage by cattle in 1992. The boulders are modern in date and not part of a larger prehistoric structure.

Site 7 Cord rig, Cawfields Farm
OS Grid Ref NY 71606636

Disturbed area of cord rig. Not visible on the ground but known from aerial photography (Newcastle University Aerial Photographs Collection NY 7166 A–O). Another potential area of cord rig might be around the south-east corner of Roman temporary camp Haltwhistle 1 (NY 76NW 13). Areas of cord rig are also known around the prehistoric settlement at Greenlee Lough just to the north of the estate (Welfare 1986, 30, 35).

Site 14 The *vicus*, Housesteads Fort

OS Grid Ref NY 79056873

The *vicus* was the civilian settlement surrounding Housesteads Fort. It is thought to have originated to the south at the bottom of the hill, but this presupposes that the Vallum acted as a military buffer zone until the late second century AD. The most extensively excavated area is that immediately south of the fort, investigated by the Durham University Excavation Committee from 1931 to 1934, an area currently under the guardianship of English Heritage. Excavations had begun on the *vicus* under Clayton, following the removal of the original farmhouse to its current position in 1863 (located on MacLauchlan's plan of the fort dated *c*.1852; cf Bruce 1867, 129). Buildings I, II, III, IV, V, VII, IX and XVI were fully excavated between 1931 and 1932 and were all consolidated with the exception of the south annexe of III and the east wall and south yard of IX. Buildings V, VII and XVI were built of fine-quality ashlar, extremely rare at sites on Hadrian's Wall, suggesting an official building. Building V has been labelled 'house of the BENIFICIARIUS CONSULARIS', a man known to have been an official on the line of the Wall, although there is no direct evidence for this. The remaining buildings in the settlement's core were located by 'a rapid tracing of the walls' (Birley and Keeney 1935, 247), and the outline of trenches for Building XIV clearly remain. This work will have disturbed the surviving stratigraphy. There is still considerable potential in the southern and western areas of the investigated *vicus*. F. G. Simpson investigated the site of a Roman limekiln to the east of the Knag Burn in 1909. Away from the core area are a number of uninvestigated earthworks, including the fourth-century enclosures to the west of the fort and sites to the south near Chapel Hill.

Site 15 *Mithraeum*, Housesteads *vicus*

OS Grid Ref NY 79076848

The temple of the popular Roman god Mithras, known as the *mithraeum*, was completely excavated by Bosanquet (1904, 255–63; cf NRO c8/41 and 48),

the west end having already been recorded by Hodgson in 1822 (1882, 273–5, Fig. 4 facing p. 263). Bosanquet's description and Gibson's photographs indicate a poor state of preservation, the east and west ends being almost obliterated, though the wooden planking and logs of the floor surface did survive in the central area (Crow 1995, 108, Fig. 71).

Site 16 Milecastle 37 (Housesteads)

OS Grid Ref NY 78506869

Milecastle 37 was originally excavated and restored by Clayton in 1853 (1855b, 269). Its poor state of preservation led to the north gate being re-excavated by Simpson in 1907 (Simpson, G. 1976, 119–23). The milecastle was excavated again by the Durham University Committee in 1933 (Blair 1934, 103 ff.). Short-axis type of milecastle measuring 17.5 m east–west and 15.1 m north–south, walls 2.7 m wide, north wall 3.04 m wide. North wall stands 2.2 m high internally with a string course, all original masonry on the south face, the side walls stand up to 1.5 m with up to 2 Roman courses surviving, the rest is rebuild. The north face of the north wall has been partly consolidated, especially around the blocked gateway, and the base of the arch over the gate has been replaced on the south face of the gateway. Further excavations conducted by Crow between 1988 and 1989 revealed 3 periods of build at the north gate: having been built it was blocked and then partly demolished. At both north and south gateways there are post holes for sets of double doors. A single barrack block in the east half survives to 1 m in height. There is much excavation spoil on the north of the milecastle blocking what would have been a difficult but possible descent to the base of the crags.

Site 17 Milecastle 38 (Hotbank)

OS Grid Ref NY 77276813

Milecastle 38 was excavated by F. G. Simpson in 1935 in order to establish its dimensions and gateway type (Birley *et al.* 1936, 263) and was found to be 18.59 m east–west by 14.9 m north–south.

Short axis with Type I gates that were later reduced to 1.2 m. The milecastle measures 18 m north-east by 17.4 m south-west internally; the north-east wall is 2.6 m wide and 1.2 m high but only robber trenches exist on the south and east sides 3.6 m wide and up to 1.4 m deep. There is a rectangular building in the south-west corner and a causeway, 3.6 m wide, lies in the east. Pottery indicated occupation up to the fourth century AD.

Site 18 Milecastle 39 (Castle Nick)
OS Grid Ref NY 76066773

Milecastle 39 (Castle Nick) was originally excavated and restored by John Clayton in 1854 (Simpson, G. 1976, 81). It was subsequently re-excavated by F. G. Simpson between 1908 and 1911 and was found to measure 18.9 m long by 15.05 m on the north side, 15.75 m across on the south side (long axis). The gates were Type II, the gate measured 2.6 m wide at the entrance and was subsequently reduced in the second century to 1.2 m wide. A building on the west side was found, 2.7 m wide and 5.6 m long. The milecastle was subsequently excavated again by Crow between 1985 and 1987. The north gate, north wall and wing foundations were built first, together with the foundations of the east wall and the butt end of the west wall; these foundations were later reduced and set in steps cut into the hill slope because of the steep slope. In earlier phases a long barrack stood on the west side with a row of small buildings on the east. Excavations in 1986 showed that the road that ran through the Milecastle was restricted to 2 m across by post holes on one side and barracks on the other. In the south-east corner was a stone oven and in the south-west corner a rectangular building with a sunken floor associated with Roman finds. The south gate was found to be of clay-bonded whinstone boulders rather than the sandstone blocks of the north gate which suggests that the south gate had no tower. The latest Roman building lay on the west side with doorways facing the east; these were then given curving porches that overlay the road. The north and south gateways were narrowed; the Milecastle appears to have been occupied until the late fourth century. In the eighteenth century a possible milking house was built in the west corner.

Site 19 Milecastle 41 (Shield-on-the-Wall)
OS Grid Ref NY 73036706

The Milecastle survives as a near square enclosure with a turf bank about 0.5 m high, but increasing up to 1.2 m high to the east externally; robber trenches are visible and there is a slight depression in the north-east corner. The Milecastle was used as an allotment for the original early eighteenth-century Shield-on-the-Wall Farm marked on the 1787 Melkridge Township Enclosure Award map (NRO 309/m.89).

Site 20 Milecastle 42 (Cawfields)
OS Grid Ref NY 71576669

Milecastle 42 lies on a steep south-facing slope, between 8 and 10 m south of the steep north-facing crags and looks over Hole Gap to the west. It measures 17.8 m east–west by 14.4 m north–south internally, with walls 2.8 m thick and 1.4 m high; the whole slopes internally north–south by 15–20 degrees. Excavations in 1936 revealed the Milecastle to be short-axis type with Type 1 gates (Birley *et al.* 1936, 269). The pivots must have been set at a higher level than the foundation slabs to enable the doors to open. The north gate is well built, jutting out north and south of the Wall line, measuring 3.4 m in width and 1.5 m in height inserted into a wall which is 2.9 m wide. The inner doorway of the north gate is 2.8 m wide, the outer doorway is 2.9 m wide and it is 3.4 m wide in the centre. The south gateway similarly juts out from the wall-line of the milecastle and survives up to 1.6 m in height. The inner doorway of the south gate is 2.7 m wide, the outer 2.9 m wide and it is 3.4 m in the centre. The east and west walls of the milecastle survive up to 1.4 m high with 5 courses of stone. Milecastle 42 was originally excavated by Clayton in 1848 (1855a, 54). It was re-excavated by Charlesworth in 1966–7 and then consolidated by the Ministry of Works (Charlesworth, 1968).

Site 21 Turret 39a (Peel Crags)

OS Grid Ref NY 75626763

Excavated by Simpson in 1911 and found to be abandoned, dismantled and its recess built up at the end of the 2nd century AD (Simpson, G. 1976, 98–107). In the south-west corner was a rectangular structure, 1.1 m by 0.84 m. In the north-west corner the burial of a man and a woman was overlaid by blocking material. The turret is visible as a slight rectangular hollow about 0.2 m deep and a slight step in the south face of the Wall. Turrets 37a (Rapishaw Gap), 37b (Hotbank), 38a (Milking Gap), 38b (Highshield Crags), 39b (Steel Rigg), 40a (Melkridge Common), 41a (Caw Gap), and 41b (Thorny Doors) were all located and investigated by Simpson between 1911 and 1912.

Site 22 The Stanegate

OS Grid Ref NY 72646626 – NY 71426607

The first-century Roman road known as the Stanegate runs across Cawfields Common, entering the estate to the east by the Mare and Foal standing stones and leaving just south of Haltwhistle Burn Fortlet. Towards the east end the road is visible as a level terrace way with a south-facing scarp. Heavily disturbed to the west by nineteenth-century iron-stone working next to the modern lane to Cawfields Quarry. Here, the Stanegate is vaguely traceable as a vegetation mark and a prominent agger, or embankment, 5.6 m wide, as it rises up on to a low ridge. The Stanegate is only one of many later trackways on the ridge and its course is difficult to trace until about the mid-point of this section, where it can be seen as an agger 7.9 m wide, with side ditches up to 1 m deep. Sections were cut by Simpson during the excavation of Haltwhistle Burn Fortlet in 1907–8, revealing a rough surface of cobbles and gravel, considerably raised in the middle immediately below the turf (Gibson and Simpson 1909, 44–6). No kerbstones were found. South of Haltwhistle Fort the Stanegate is visible as a low bank but it increases to form a prominent agger 5.6 m wide with ditch sides, up to 2.2 m high on the south side on the more level ground south of

the fortlet. It has been disturbed and is difficult to trace between the south-east corner of the fortlet and the junction with the field wall. The Stanegate remained in use throughout the medieval period until it was replaced by the Military Road in the 1750s.

Site 23 Roman watermill, Cawfields Farm

OS Grid Ref NY 71136654

Situated at a point between the Wall and the Vallum, on the south bank of the Haltwhistle Burn, the Roman watermill was excavated by Simpson in 1907 and was found to be a nearly rectangular building measuring 6.98 m by 4.8 m and containing fragments of millstones, hand mills, pottery and a Roman coin, now in Chesters Museum. The site was infilled after excavation and the only visible remains are some exposed Roman masonry, up to 4 courses, facing the burn. Simpson concluded that the building of the watermill dated to around AD 225 and was destroyed sometime after AD 270 (Simpson, G. 1976, 32–43).

Site 24 Haltwhistle Burn Fort

OS Grid Ref NY 71446615

Trajanic fort with stone-faced earthen ramparts and stone-built interior buildings, enclosed within a larger, irregular ditch. Excavated by Simpson in 1907–8, it was revealed to measure 64 m east–west by 52 m north–south and to contain at least 1 barrack, a centurion's quarters, a small administrative building, a store and a part-walled yard accompanying it (Gibson and Simpson 1909, 1–72). Some of the interior features can still be traced today. There are entrances on the east and south sides with well-preserved gateways and causeways across the ditch.

Site 25 Cawfields Common temporary camps

OS Grid Ref NY 71506640

At the west end of Cawfields Common, on either side of the Haltwhistle Burn, is a group of 5 temporary Roman camps, with another just north of the Wall by Cawfields farmhouse. The ramparts of another camp lie just within the boundaries of the Trust's estate at Milecastle House to the south-east, and another lies off the estate to the south-west. Their function is not fully understood; they are probably of a later date than the Haltwhistle Burn Fortlet, but could have been occupied by troops constructing the fort at Great Chesters (Aesica). Alternatively, they may have been thrown up as practice camps for underemployed soldiers stationed at the fort in times of relative quiet. Certainly, one shows evidence of being reduced in size by a half following the original construction (Haltwhistle Camps 2 and 3), whilst another on the west side of the burn (Markham Cottage Camp 1) was reduced to a fraction of its earlier size at a later date. The size of the camps differs greatly: the largest is Markham Cottage Camp 1, whose boundaries measure 460 m north–south by 365 m east–west, enclosing an area of 16.8 ha (41.5 acres). Haltwhistle Burn Camp 1, by comparison, covers an area of only 1 ha (2.5 acres), and Haltwhistle Burn Camps 1 and 2 less than 0.7 hectares (1.7 acres). The smallest camp is Haltwhistle Burn Camp 4, measuring 19 m east–west by 16 m traversely, enclosing an area of 0.002 ha (0.0049 acres). Its size alone surely meant that it had little strategic importance, and could only have served as a practice camp. None of these camps has been fully excavated; Simpson and Gibson investigated the south-east angle of Haltwhistle Camp 1 in 1908, revealing that the walls were constructed of turf, but no dating material was found. Haltwhistle Burn Camps 2 and 3 overlie an area of prehistoric cord rig cultivation. The forts to the west of the burn have been greatly disturbed by post-medieval ridge and furrow.

Medieval and post-medieval sites

Site 26 Bradley Green deserted medieval village
OS Grid Ref NY 777674

Bradley Green lies in a field on the south-facing slope of a hill leading down to the Bradley Burn and is noted for its medieval and post-medieval remains, known as a deserted medieval village.

The settlement is largely made up of long and narrow, or strip, fields containing marks known as ridge and furrow. Their broad width, up to 7 m in places, together with their 'inverted-S'-shaped ridge endings, clearly indicate that they are medieval in date. A number of earthwork enclosures, some of which may be building platforms, can be seen within the deserted medieval village. An incised trackway runs down the west side and is possibly medieval. The field has been much quarried, presumably for wall- and road-building material. A collapsed late eighteenth-century Enclosure-period wall runs north through the site. On the 5th and 6th September 1306 Edward I stayed at Bradley Hall on his way along the Stanegate to Carlisle during his final Scottish campaign (Hodgson 1840, 326). It is believed that the medieval remains at Bradley Green were occupied by the bondsmen of the owner of Bradley Hall in the late thirteenth to early fourteenth century. Occupation was short-lived, however, as climatic deterioration and the Black Death brought about an end to the permanent occupation of the uplands of Britain in the mid-fourteenth century.

Site 27 Bogle Hole shielings
OS Grid Ref NY 72956693

Line of 4 or possibly more shielings, rectangular turf-covered stone structures, the largest of which lies at the east end of the Bogle Hole. The average dimensions are 5 m long and 2.3 m wide with walls up to 0.4 m high.

Site 28 Group of shielings on Mons Fabricius
OS Grid Ref NY 76106775

A group of 4 shielings, excavated by Crow between 1985 and 1986, built up against the south face of Hadrian's Wall. They were rectangular in plan with unmortared rubble-stone walls and each had been repaired and rebuilt a number of times. The earliest pottery found dated to the fourteenth century, but later flagged floors and hearths could be dated to the early sixteenth century. A distinct trackway led up to the shielings around the side of the hill.

Another group of shielings is known scattered about the lower slopes of the hill. Dimensions are as follows: 1: west end, south-east corner and west end survive but half of west side is missing, up to 3 courses (0.4 m) high, 6.3 m by 3.6 m. 2: fragmentary remains surviving up to 1 course high. 3: east end, 2-cell shieling, 6.9 m by 2.6 m, up to 2 courses high. The interior of the west half is paved. The shielings have been consolidated and are on display to visitors.

Site 29 Group of shielings at the base of Mons Fabricius

OS Grid Ref NY 761676

Clustered around the lower slopes of Mons Fabricius and over the ruins of Milecastle 39 is a scattered group of 7 shielings. They are constructed of unmortared rubble and unhewn whinstone, with walls up to 1 m wide and up to 0.4 m high, and would probably have been topped with a turf roof (Ramm *et al.* 1970, 1–10). One of the shielings was investigated by Crow during excavations south of Milecastle 39 in 1986, but very few finds were found and it is uncertain whether these shielings are contemporary with those on top of Mons Fabricius, which can be dated to between the fourteenth and sixteenth centuries.

Site 30 Steel Rigg peel tower, East Bog Farm

OS Grid Ref NY 75226756

Site of a fourteenth- to fifteenth-centuryBorder peel tower, after which Peel Gap is named. No structural remains of the tower survive but the site is visible as a slight platform measuring 6.2 m by 6.5 m surrounded by excavation trenches. Traces of foundations are visible. The site was excavated by F. G. Simpson in 1909, revealing fragments of green-glazed glass dating to the fourteenth century (Simpson, G. 1976, 109). One of Simpson's spoil heaps lies to the south.

Site 31 King's Wicket enclosure, Hotbank Farm

OS Grid Ref NY 798695

King's Wicket is the name of the wicket gate in the line of Hadrian's Wall in Busy Gap. The enclosure is a large triangular earthwork formed by an earthen bank with a superficial ditch, based on the Wall-ditch. A possible entrance lies at the north-west corner. The feature is thought to be a stock enclosure associated with a traditional drove road running through the Wall at this point. The date is uncertain, but in the late Middle Ages Busy Gap was a notorious haunt for bandits and raiders, known as 'Busy Gap rogues', and the stock held in the enclosure may not always have been there with the owner's consent (Bruce 1881, 137–8).

Site 32 Steel Rigg farmstead, Hotbank Farm

OS Grid Ref NY 758680

The remains at Steel Rigg Farm consist of a number of hedge banks, collapsed boulder walls and relics of stone-clad banks. Narrow ridge and furrow can be seen on Steel Rigg and on the opposite slope to the north. The land in the middle possibly represents wet pasture and the walls and hedges were used to separate livestock from crops. The remains of an enclosure (possibly the site of the original farmstead) is situated along the inside of a large hedge bank running east–west that seems to have formed the north boundary of the farm. The first record of a farm at Steel Rigg is a lease agreement dated to 1698, which describes the farm's exterior boundaries and the crops grown within them, including corn and grain (NRO ZBL 1/100). Within the farm boundaries is a stack stand used for the storing of feed, and surrounded by an earthwork bank 8m in diameter, designed to exclude animals. The farm is marked on the Allgood version of the 1749 map of the proposed Military Road showing hedge boundaries and ridge and furrow, all of which can be seen on the ground and were surveyed by Crow between 1985 and 1987. The area is marked on the 1793 Enclosure Acts map for the township of Henshaw as being 'anciently inclosed' (NRO 309/m. 71) suggesting that by this time the farm was well established or may have even gone out of use by then. The farmhouse was moved from its original position to a new one on the site of what is now the Steel Rigg car-park around 1750. That farmhouse was demolished by John Clayton between 1866 and 1898.

Site 33 Housesteads bastle house

OS Grid Ref NY 78996880

On the south side of the south gate of Housesteads Fort is a post-Roman building identified as a post-medieval bastle (Whitworth 1990, 8; Ryder 1990, 11–12). It was cleared in the nineteenth century with the rest of the south gate. Within the guard chamber is a drying kiln entered from the lower room of the bastle. This has been removed and then replaced to allow the guard-chamber walls to be consolidated. In 1984 the custodian's hut was removed allowing the interior walls to be seen more clearly: internal splayed vents survive in the south, east and west walls. Note that the vent in the north wall of the guard chamber is original and appears on photographs taken before consolidation. No trace survives of the oven shown on Hodgson's plan on the north-east side, (Birley 1937–8, Fig. 3). His plan also shows an apron of flagging in the angle of the east wall of the guard chamber and the Roman wall. Fragments of this flagging can be seen in a Simpson photograph of the south curtain excavations (NRO FGS 8/41). Steps are shown leading up to the drying kiln from this flagged area (Bruce 1867, 146). The only possible surviving feature of this work is the steps leading up to the Roman wall, in the angle formed with the guard chamber. The stairway leading from the south, on the east side of the bastle, is a secondary addition. The north half of the stair-way has been removed, possibly when the bastle and guard chamber were cleared out by Hodgson and Clayton. Although they are not shown on Hodgson's plan, stairs are marked in this position by Bosanquet (1904 282–3, Fig. 42, Pl. 19). It was then buried by a turf-covered retaining wall 1.30 to 2.20 m wide, which extended the length of the bastle east wall to its junction with the fort south curtain. A base of rubble packing underlay the stairs and extended up to and over the south curtain (cf the stone flagging

recorded by Hodgson (Birley 1937–8, 183, Fig. 3)). The east retaining wall was removed during this consolidation to expose the stairway and the east wall. The bastle house is likely to have been built by the notorious reiving family, the Armstrongs, in the seventeenth century.

Site 34 Bastle house, Bradley Green deserted medieval village

OS Grid Ref NY 779676

Site of a bastle house, late sixteenth or early seventeenth century, measuring 14.3 m east–west by 6.3 m. Large quarried cornerstones survive at south-west, north-west, north-east. Turf-covered quarried stone walls up to 0.8 m wide and 0.6 m high internally. There is an entrance at the west end of the south face with one door-frame stone still *in situ* and another lying just outside. Collapsed drystone walls run off east and west from south corners of the feature. It is slightly unusual in that the ground-floor entrance was in the centre of the south-facing long wall and not in a gable, but in other respects conforms precisely to bastle specifications. The feature is labelled 'Greenbyer (ruin)' on the 1st Edition Ordnance Survey map of 1866 (sheet LXXXIII). Bastle houses are rarely found alone and another possible bastle lies to the east.

Site 35 Stack stand north of Housesteads Fort (Fairy Stone)

OS Grid Ref NY 79006895

Subcircular raised platform 7.2 m north-east–south-west by 5.6 m internally, banks 2.5 m wide and 0.3 m high. The entrance is at the north-east and mea-sures 1 m wide. A second stack stand lies 1.5 m to the north-west. The near-recumbent stone measures 1 m long, 0.41 m wide and 0.14 m thick. Hodgson observed the feature in the early nineteenth century (1822, 270) and it was recorded by MacLauchlan in 1852 and has been marked on OS maps as 'Fairy Stone' since the first edition in 1866. R. E. Birley (1962, 127–8) mentions Hodgson's account but describes a different circular structure, probably that 260 m west-north-west of Housesteads Fort.

Site 36 Ridge and furrow at Highshield Farm

OS Grid Ref NY 765671

South of the Military Road, traces of ridge and furrow can be seen running north–south down the south-facing slope, enclosed by hedge-bank boundaries that clearly predate the drystone walls. The ridges are quite straight and the furrows measure, on average, 3.1 m apart. The cultivated area is overlaid by a drystone wall at the east end and extends slightly into OS Field Parcel 8227. The ridge and furrow is post-medieval in date (Taylor 1975, 126) and is probably contemporary with the original late seventeenth-century farmhouse at Highshield. Aerial photographs show further areas of ridge and furrow to the west (Newcastle University Aerial Photograph Collection AP NY 7667/1; NY 7667/11) but they are less clear on the ground. That to the west is very narrow and may date from the period of the wars with France (1799–1815), when an increasing demand for corn briefly brought marginal upland areas into cultivation (Taylor 1975, 143).

Site 37 Ridge and furrow at Bradley Farm

OS Grid Ref NY 774680

To the east of the farmhouse at Bradley is an area of well-defined ridge and furrow. To the west of the field the ridge and furrow is quite wide, over 5 m between furrows, and the ridge ends appear slightly curved at the ends, like an inverted 'S'. The ridges resemble cultivation terraces, or strip lynchets, laid out running down the slope as opposed to the usual form running along the line of the contours. The ridge and furrow is similar to that at Bradley Green, which is known to be medieval and so may be of the same date. To the east of the field the ridge and furrow is narrower, with furrows on average 3.8 m apart, and is more likely to be post-medieval in date (Taylor 1975, 126) or at least to overlie earlier cultivation.

Industrial sites

Site 38 Sow kilns on Cawfields Common

OS Grid Ref NY 72006650

Known from aerial photographs (Newcastle University Aerial Photograph Collection NY 7166 A–O). Noted by Hedley in the 1930s (Hedley 1936, 307). Primitive sort of limekiln for agricultural use. No stone used in construction but kiln was formed by scooping out a circular hollow on the hillside with one side open to the fall of the hill (Jobey 1966, 2). Another sow kiln was identified by Simpson south of Cawfields Quarry by the north mound of the Vallum in 1908 (Simpson, G. 1976, 116).

Site 39 Bradley Green corn-drying kiln

OS Grid Ref NY 77857651

Built into the slope overlooking Bradley Burn, circular in shape with an opening facing north-west. The interior walls are constructed of quarried and undressed stone with no evidence of mortar and stand up to 1 m high internally and 1.04 m wide on the south-west. Probably early eighteenth century (Ramm *et al.* 1970, 44–6).

Site 40 Cuddy's Crags limekiln

OS Grid Ref NY 779693

Ruined limekiln. Exterior in good condition, east-facing wall, 3.8 m in height, with 2 draw arches, 2.65 m in height, arrowhead and rounded corners in elevation, one eye per arch. One rectangular pot, 5.43 m by 10.97. The roof has collapsed and the interior is partly filled with rubble. Earth is banked up against the west wall to the level of the roof to allow limestone to be easily tipped into the burning pot. There are limestone quarries to the east and the west of the limekiln.

Site 41 Bradley Farm limekiln

OS Grid Ref NY 782683

Limekiln with 2 draw arches (arrowhead). Quarried stone and reused material from Hadrian's Wall. Draw arch faces south. Oval-shaped brick-lined flume on top. The interior pot is partly filled with nineteenth- and early twentieth-century debris, pottery, glass bottles, scraps of iron. The limekiln was consolidated by the National Trust in 1983. There is a limestone quarry associated with the limekiln immediately to the north.

Site 42 Mine shaft, Shield-on-the-Wall Farm

OS Grid Ref NY 72806652

The mine shaft survives as a circular earthwork 15 m in diameter, 1.05 m in height with a slight depression in the middle. The shaft itself has been filled in. It probably dates from between 1790 and 1810, the great period of land improvement and limeburning, when coal was needed for firing the kilns. It is associated with the limekiln and other shafts on the south side of the Military Road (now the B6318).

Site 43 Ironstone quarry and trackways, Cawfields Common

OS Grid Ref NY 71556604

The quarry was probably opened in 1856, the same year that a blast furnace began production at the Haltwhistle Ironworks. Ironstone was taken from the quarry and weathered for many months on the open ground before being calcined in great heaps with poor-quality coal (Raistrick 1973, 54). A trackway carried the quarried ironstone along a raised bank with a levelled surface that runs from the south-east corner of OS Field Parcel 2032 on the west side of the lane leading to Cawfields car-park. It is cut by the lane and reappears on the east side in OS Field Parcel 0048, where it has been disturbed by later quarrying. Its condition improves as it runs around the outside of the ironstone quarry and stops in the middle of the quarry itself. It probably dates from the same time as the quarry, c.1856, and was used to carry ironstone down the Haltwhistle Burn wagonway to Haltwhistle Ironstone Works. Marked on the 1st Edition Ordnance Survey map of 1866 (sheet LXXXIII). The surviving trackway stands at 0.3 m high and 1.4 m wide across the top. The wagonway has been dismantled and no tracks survive.

Site 44 Cawfields Whinstone Quarry

OS Grid Ref NY 71406658

The quarry was opened in 1902 to provide whinstone for construction work (Richmond 1944, 77–8). During the time of its operation the Whin Sill was demolished from Burnhead cottage to Hole Gap, just west of Milecastle 42, taking with it not only Hadrian's Wall but also what may have been a medieval building discovered by Simpson in 1907 (Simpson, G. 1976, 80). After quarrying ceased in 1952 the site was infilled with the spoil from the ironstone quarry on Cawfields Common and is now partly flooded.

Site 45 Haltwhistle Burn trackway, Cawfields Farm

OS Grid Ref NY 71116660 to NY 71406607

The wagonway survives as a raised platform, averaging 8 m wide, 0.75 m high, running alongside the Haltwhistle Burn from the road bridge by Cawfields Quarry to the bridge carrying the B6318, the estate boundary. Built as an extension to the nineteenth-century Haltwhistle Burn wagonway that serviced industries located down the burn (Storey 1973, 56). The Cawfields Whinstone Quarry opened in 1902 and closed in 1952 and whinstone was taken along the wagonway down the Haltwhistle Burn to the railway in the South Tyne valley. No trackway survives today and the bank has been partly covered with slump from the steep slope on the east side of the burn.

Site 46 Shield-on-the-Wall Whinstone Quarry

OS Grid Ref NY 72856685

The announcement in 1930 that the Whin Sill was to be demolished from Caw Gap to Housesteads, and Hadrian's Wall along with it, caused great controversy (Richmond 1944, 77–8). Quarrying was therefore restricted to the south side of the Whin Sill and took part of the Military Way with it. Quarrying was finally stoped in 1942. The quarry is visible as a deep cutting into the Whin Sill north-east of the farmhouse.

Site 47 Loaning Head freestone quarry, East Bog Farm

OS Grid Ref NY 752669

Open-cast quarry. Probably dates to the building of the Military Road in the 1750s and is known from the 1783 Enclosure Award map for Henshaw Township (NRO 309/m.71). To the west of the road to Steel Rigg the quarrying greatly disturbed the north mound and berm of the Vallum. The quarry is partly enclosed on the north side by a disused hedge bank. To the east the quarrying is contained on the south side by the north mound of the Vallum and a hedge bank to the east. The quarry seems to post-date the building of the lane leading to Steel Rigg, which is visible on the 1749 map of the proposed Military Road (Allgood version).

Farmhouses and cottages

Site 48 Cawfields farmhouse
OS Grid Ref NY 71686700

The first records for a farmhouse at Cawfields date back to 1696, when the farm was occupied by the Hutchinson family (Haltwhistle parish records). The current farmhouse at Cawfields, however, probably dates from the mid-eighteenth century but was extensively remodelled by John Clayton after he purchased it in 1848. Further extensions have been added in the last 20 years. The farmhouse, along with a collection of stores and outhouses, make up the main yard. The farmhouse is on an L-shape plan with gabled ends and a gabled kitchen return. The front façade, which faces Cawfields Crags, is built of random sandstone rubble, the windows are dressed with smooth sandstone, as are the external angles of the wall. Cornices adorn the gabled ends of the houses and porch, typical of Clayton's farm buildings.

Site 49 East Cawfields farmhouse

OS Grid Ref NY 71876727

East Cawfields farmhouse probably dates from the mid-eighteenth century and contains twentieth-century modern additions to the rear of the house. It lies on an L-shaped axis facing Cawfields Crags north-east of Cawfields Farm. The south-west façade consists of a farmhouse with a two-tiered shed attached (National Trust Vernacular Buildings Survey HW/3/2). Cawfields was bought by John Clayton in 1873 but does not show any of the neo-Tudor characteristics of other Clayton farm buildings in the Trust's estate.

Site 50 Shield-on-the-Wall farmhouse

OS Grid Ref NY 72686665

The mid-nineteenth-century farmhouse at Shield-on-the-Wall was built by John Clayton to replace the original farmhouse that lay on the line of Hadrian's Wall at Milecastle 41. The farm was purchased by Clayton in 1848 from Robert Dixon for £1,200 (NRO 2219/55). Between 1866 and 1886 Clayton demolished the original farmhouse to leave the milecastle, which had been used as an allotment, free and prevent further stone-robbing from the Wall. The new farm was built down off the hill immediately south of the Vallum. The exact date of the building of the new farm is not certain, but it must have taken place before 1886, when it was referred to in the *Bulmer's Directory* of that year as 'Shield *off* the Wall'. It had reverted back to its old name, however, by 1896 when the 2nd Edition Ordnance Survey map was published. Its mullioned windows, square corbels and carved kneelers are characteristic of Clayton buildings found throughout the Trust's estate (National Trust Vernacular Buildings Survey HW/1/6).

Site 51 East Bog farmhouse

OS Grid Ref NY 74756717

East Bog farm, originally known simply as The
Bogg, probably first evolved as a linear steading.
The earliest mention of The Bogg is in a decree of
Charles II in 1664, when it was occupied by a
Mr Thomas Ridley (NRO 1888/35/27). The central
sector of the farmhouse probably dates back to the
late eighteenth century. Expansion of the farm took
place in the mid-nineteenth century after it had
been purchased by John Clayton in 1851, along with
land at Pasture Head (Once Brewed). By 1860 the
double-fronted house had been added on to the
eighteenth-century steading and an L-shaped range
of farm buildings was added, all displaying the
distinctive carved kneelers characteristic of Clayton's
buildings along the Wall. The hay shed with stone
piers and inner columns was added to the north
side in the last quarter of the nineteenth century
and a cart shed and byre were built to enclose the
south side of the farmyard before the Chesters
estate was divided into lots and sold in 1929
(Sale Cat. CLAs 148).

Site 52 Hotbank farmhouse

OS Grid Ref NY 77246818

Imposing double-pile farmhouse, the two service
rooms of which comprised the eighteenth-century
farmhouse. Two new parlours were added to the
front before 1837, which pre-dated the building of
the L-shaped arrangement of the farm buildings.
Its position in the incline between Crag Lough and
Hotbank Crags, immediately north of Milecastle 38,
suggests it was built largely of Roman stone. An
early map of the area (NRO ZCL/C/160), probably
drawn in the early nineteenth century, shows
Hotbank as a linear steading with access only from
the north. John Clayton purchased the farm in
conjunction with Sir Robert Ingram in 1837 and
between then and 1860 the L-plan arrangement of
farm buildings adjoining the north-east gable of the
farmhouse was demolished and the farmyard moved
to the back of the farmhouse. Clayton bought up
Ingram's share of the farm in 1861 for £4,200

(NRO ZHA 1/4), but it seems that it had already
been enlarged and improved before then as it
shares none of the characteristics found on other
Clayton buildings in the estate. In c.1900, a hay
barn was built on the north-west side of the range.
Otherwise, few additions or alterations have been
made since 1860 (National Trust Vernacular
Buildings Survey HW/1/4).

Site 53 Bradley farmhouse

OS Grid Ref NY 77626797

The first record of a farmstead at Bradley dates
back to the marriage of Cuthbert Dixon of 'High
Bradley' in 1712, and the Dixons were to remain
tenants of the Blackett family until the end of the
eighteenth century. The farmstead is marked on the
map of the Roman Wall drawn by John Horsley in
1732. The current farmhouse at Bradley probably
dates from the mid- to late eighteenth century.
The land around Bradley was enclosed after an Act
of Parliament in 1783 (NRO 309/m.71) and it is
possible the farmhouse dates from about that time.
The farm remained in the hands of the Blackett
family until it was donated to the National Trust by
R. E. F. Cely-Trevellian in 1975, and so does not
display any of the characteristics of a Clayton farm
building, such as carved kneelers or mullioned
windows.

Site 54 Highshield farmhouse

OS Grid Ref NY 76686721

In 1860, Highshield was comprised of two linear
steadings originally dating back to c.1700 on either
side of the farm track – East and West High Shield.
Highshield had long been in the ownership of the
Blackett family. Simon Wilkinson of Highshield
signed the General Release on the 9th March 1745
(NRO ZBL 25/2) and the farm was rebuilt during the
time of Sir Edward Blackett, Baronet, in the late
eighteenth century. It never formed part of John
Clayton's estate and so does not display the
characteristic carved kneelers and mullioned
windows. Between 1860 and 1895 West High Shield
was demolished (apart from Building 2, the pigsty/

henhouse) and a new farmhouse was built on the site in a style typical of the late-Victorian era. One small building was demolished at East High Shield but the house remained roofed until at least 1922. The house at East High Shield has now fallen into ruin and only the byre still stands.

Site 55 Peel Bothy

OS Grid Ref NY 75256743

Peel Bothy, built to house a hinde, or farmworker, replaced a cottage much closer to Hadrian's Wall in Peel Gap. It seems to date from the 1850s, when John Clayton relocated a series of farm buildings on his estate away from the line of the Wall, eg Shield-on-the-Wall. The cottage is built of local rubble with more regular dressing to the opening and corners. The rendered finish, though not unknown in local buildings, appears in this case to be a recent treatment. The neo-Tudor style, typical of Clayton's buildings, is most apparent here in the projecting porch with its pointed doorway and shouldered gables. The cottage originally had 2 rooms with hearths, and a byre and hay shed attached to the east gable. Later improvements included a scullery to the north, and a free-standing Netty and fuel stove with set-pot.

Site 56 Housesteads farmhouse

OS Grid Ref NY 78906862

On the 2nd February 1838 John Clayton purchased Housesteads for £6,900 from Thomas Gibson, George Gibson and others (NRO ZHA 1/2). Between 1860 and 1896 the small linear steading just outside the south gate (Bruce 1921, 153) was replaced by a neo-Tudor farmhouse and farm buildings 100 m to the south-west. Clayton's new farmhouse evoked the sixteenth century and was cruciform in plan with narrow slit windows, tall octagonal chimneys, stone finials on the gables, hood-mountings above all the windows and a mullioned window on the south, unusual in Northumberland upland farms. It is said that Clayton used the front living-room as his own personal office. The farmhouse has been occupied by the estate warden since 1984. The neat U-shaped range of farm buildings to the north is built in a similar style to the farmhouse and is currently being used as an office and an education room.

Site 57 Longside Farm building, Hotbank Farm

OS Grid Ref NY 76466841

The first mention of a farmstead known as Longside or Loughside was in 1698, when a lease agreement between William Lowes of Crowhall and Sir Edward Blackett concerning Steel Rigg refers to a property called 'Loughhead or Loughside', already owned by William Lowes (NRO ZBL 100/1). Steel Rigg, Foul Bog and Loughside or head were typical of the small farmsteads found in the upland areas of Tynedale in the late seventeenth and early eighteenth centuries, when shielding was rapidly being replaced by permanent occupation (Ramm *et al.* 1970, 44–6). The 1749 Allgood version of the proposed Military Road map marks 2 buildings just north of Crag Lough as 'Loch Houses' and the 1783 Henshaw Township Enclosures Act map marks the property similarly just north of the lough in land owned by William Burrows (NRO 309/m. 71). The land was bought up by John Clayton in 1834 along with Hotbank, Foul Bog and Steel Rigg (NRO 2219/57). The 1866 1st Edition Ordnance Survey map (sheet LXXXIII) reveals that the building had been moved from its original position and another rebuilt to the north, retaining its name 'Loughside'. The building is now known as 'Longside' (OS NY 7668, 1972 edition) and is used as a farm building by the tenant of Hotbank Farm. It is a linear stone-built byre with tiled sloping roof and a door at the east end of the south-facing long side. It has recently been restored by the National Trust. The building to the north is a modern barn.

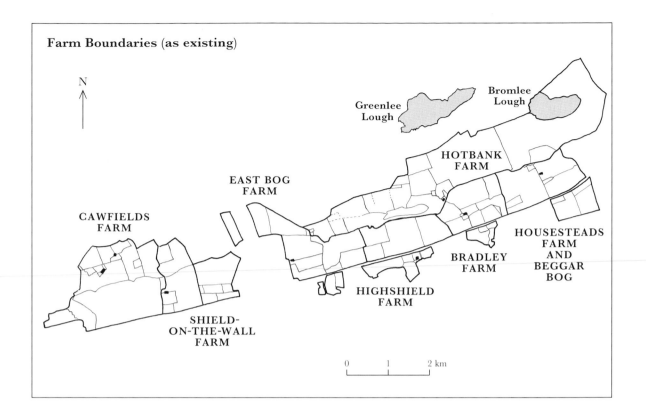

Farm Boundaries (as existing)

N

Greenlee Lough

Bromlee Lough

HOTBANK FARM

EAST BOG FARM

CAWFIELDS FARM

HOUSESTEADS FARM AND BEGGAR BOG

BRADLEY FARM

HIGHSHIELD FARM

SHIELD-ON-THE-WALL FARM

0   1   2 km

FIGURE 61 Map showing existing farm boundaries on the National Trust Hadrian's Wall estate. (R. Woodside)

Field boundaries and Enclosure Acts
(Figure 61)

1 Hotbank Farm

The original boundaries of Hotbank Farm date back to the late seventeenth century and the original farmsteads known as Hodbank, Loughside, Foulbog and Steel Rigg. The post-medieval landscape was largely unenclosed, with the exception of hedge-bank boundaries around the farmhouses and their fields (Taylor 1975, 126). All the land in the eastern half of the farm north of Hadrian's Wall between NY 76716860 and NY 79927000 lies in the Civil Parish of Bardon Mill which, prior to boundary changes in 1973, was known as Ridley Common.

In 1751 it was largely owned by the Blackett family of Matfen, who enclosed it by private agreement (NRO ZBL 4/7; Hoskins 1955, 177–95; Taylor 1975, 139–53). No map was made of the enclosures but the Tithe map of 1844 (NRO DT 393 M) reveals that enclosure had been limited and that OS Field Parcels only came into being between 1866 and 1898, as seen on the 1st and 2nd edition enclosure maps. The western part of the farm between NY 75006775 and NY 76716860 lies within Henshaw Township and was enclosed by an Act of Parliament in 1783 during the reign of George III (NRO ZBL 268/1), overlying an earlier seventeenth-century farmstead. Maps between 1866 (1st Edition Ordnance Survey map, sheet LXXXIII) and the present day reveal that the field system has changed little in over 100 years.

2 Bradley Farm

The field walls and boundaries of Bradley Farm date back to the early eighteenth century and the original farmstead known as 'High Braidley'. The post-medieval landscape was largely unenclosed, with the exception of hedge banks around small linear farmhouses and their fields (Taylor 1975, 126). A relict field boundary running east–west north of Deafley Rig, probably associated with the early eighteenth-century farmstead at Housesteads, appears to have formed the farm boundary before the building of the Military Road in the 1750s. Thorngrafton Township was enclosed by Act of Parliament in 1797 (NRO ZRI 52/17; Hoskins 1955, 177–95; Taylor 1975, 139–53) and new drystone walls were built at right angles to the Military Road completed by General Wade by 1757, overlying many of the earlier hedge-bank boundaries. The boundaries of the farm are clearly marked on the 1797 Enclosures Act map (NRO QRA 65/1) and the Tithe map of 1844 (DT 446M). However, there is no record of any field walls until the 1st Edition Ordnance Survey map of 1866 (sheet LXXXIII).

3 Beggar Bog

Beggar Bog boundaries date from the Thorngrafton Township Enclosure Act awarded by Parliament in 1797 (NRO 2860/7; Hoskins 1955, 177–95; Taylor 1975, 139–53) as laid out in the accompanying survey map (NRO QRA 50). The boundaries are predominantly drystone walls, in conditions ranging from good to totally collapsed, but modern barbed-wire fences have become more widely used in the second half of this century. The internal field walls appear to be more recent in date as they do not appear on either the 1st or 2nd Edition Ordnance Survey maps of 1866 and 1898 respectively.

4 Highshield Farm

The original boundaries of Highshield Farm date back to the late seventeenth century, when the original farmstead was occupied by the Lowes family (Haltwhistle parish records). The post-medieval landscape was largely unenclosed, with

the exception of hedge banks around small linear farmhouses and their fields. The Henshaw Township Enclosure Act map of 1783 indicates that the area of Highshield Farm was even then 'anciently inclosed land' (NRO 309/m. 71). In 1755 the Military Road cut the farm in two north and south and in 1783 Henshaw Township was enclosed by Act of Parliament (NRO ZBL 284/1; Hoskins 1955, 177–95; Taylor 1975, 139–53) and new drystone walls were built at right angles to the Military Road, overlying many of the earlier hedge-bank boundaries. The pattern of field walls on the south side of the Military Road has changed little since 1866 (1st Edition Ordnance Survey map, sheet LXXXIII).

5 East Bog Farm

The original boundaries of East Bog Farm date back to the late seventeenth century and the original farmstead known then as The Bogg. The post-medieval landscape lay largely unenclosed, with the exception of hedge banks around small linear farmhouses and their fields of narrow ridge and furrow (Taylor 1975, 126). The Henshaw Township Enclosure Act map of 1783 indicates that the area of East Bog Farm was 'anciently enclosed' (NRO 309/m. 71). Henshaw Township was enclosed by Act of Parliament in 1783 (NRO ZBL 284/1; Hoskins 1955, 177–95; Taylor 1975, 139–53) and new drystone walls were built at right angles to the Military Road completed by General Wade by 1757, overlying many of the earlier hedge-bank boundaries. By 1898, the pattern of field walls had taken on much of its current appearance (2nd Edition Ordnance Survey map, sheet LXXXIII) and only minor alterations have occurred since then.

6 Shield-on-the-Wall Farm

The boundaries of Shield-on-the-Wall Farm date to the early eighteenth century and the original farmstead on the site of Milecastle 41. Melkridge Township was enclosed by Act of Parliament in 1787 (NRO QRD 7; Hoskins 1955, 177–95; Taylor 1975, 139–53) and the accompanying map (NRO 309/m. 89) indicates that the land was divided up into a number of different allotments owned by a large number of people. Sometime between 1866 and 1886 the farmhouse was moved from the milecastle to its present position and by 1898 the field pattern was well established (2nd Edition Ordnance Survey map, sheet LXXXIII), and has changed little since then.

7 Cawfields Farm

The original boundaries of Cawfields Farm date back to the original late seventeenth-century farmstead, whose position is not known but is most likely to be around the site of the present-day farmhouse. The late seventeenth- to early eighteenth-century landscape was largely unenclosed, with the exception of hedge-bank boundaries around the small linear farmhouses and their fields of narrow ridge and furrow. Haltwhistle Common, including Cawfields Farm, was enclosed by Act of Parliament between 1804 and 1844 (NRO 691/1/16; Hoskins 1955, 177–95; Taylor 1975, 139–53). A number of notable relict earthwork boundaries can be seen at Cawfields; one, up to 1 m high and 1.6 m wide, runs north-east–south-west across the western half of OS Field Parcel 2032, cutting across the south-east corner of Roman temporary camp Markham

Cottage 2 and continuing into the next field out of the estate. Aerial photographs reveal the boundary continuing for some distance to the south, seemingly oblivious to roads and field boundaries. It is probably medieval or post-medieval and its purpose is uncertain as it does not appear to be a parish or township boundary. Another relict wall runs along the line of the ancient township boundary between Haltwhistle and Melkridge laid down in 1744 ((34) NRO ZBL 1/102) and marked on the 1787 Melkridge Township Enclosure Act map (NRO 309/m.89). Best seen just north of Hadrian's Wall on Cawfields Crags, the boundary has been retained as the modern civil parish boundary. New drystone walls were built, many overlying earlier hedge-bank boundaries, in the early nineteenth century. Unlike Thorngrafton, Henshaw and Melkridge townships, no map was drawn of the Haltwhistle enclosures but a 1930s' tracing of the 1844 Tithe Award map (NRO 2588) appears to mark the field boundaries north of Hadrian's Wall prior to enclosure. By 1898, however, the pattern of field walls had assumed the form it takes today (2nd Edition Ordnance Survey map, sheets LXXXIII SW and XCII NW).

Early Modern 1700–1900

The Early Modern period sees the first move towards the permanent settlement of the estate. New farms are established and the area is enclosed with drystone walls by Acts of Parliament passed in the late eighteenth century. The land surrounding Hadrian's Wall is bought up by John Clayton of Chesters from 1834. Antiquaries and tourists begin to visit the Wall and publish their findings.

1702
Christopher Hunter visits Housesteads.

1708–9
Robert Smith visits Housesteads and the Wall.

1716
Warburton publishes his map of the Wall.

1724
Alexander Gordon and Sir John Clerk visit the middle lengths of the Wall and Housesteads.

1725
William Stukeley visits Housesteads.

1730
John Horsley visits Hadrian's Wall and two years later publishes *Britannia Romana*.

1751
Act of Parliament passed allowing General Wade to build the Military Road between Newcastle and Carlisle following Jacobite Rebellion. Ridley Common enclosed by private agreement.

1753
Warburton publishes *Vallum Romanorum*.

1769
New edition of Camden's *Britannia* edited by Gough.

1776
Stukeley publishes *Iter Boreale* of 1725 in *Itinerarium Curiosum*.

1783–93
Henshaw, Melkridge and Thorngrafton Township Enclosure Acts awarded by Parliament.

1793–1815
Wars with France encourage intensive cultivation throughout the upland regions of Northumberland.

1801
William Hutton and John Skinner both independently walk the Wall.

1807
Dr John Lingard walks the Wall.

1813
Society of Antiquaries of Newcastle upon Tyne founded. In 1821 it acquires George Gibson's collection of inscriptions from Housesteads.

1822
John Hodgson begins excavations at Housesteads Fort and the *mithraeum* at Housesteads.

1830–3
Hodgson returns to Housesteads to excavate the south, east and west gates.

1835–48
John Clayton begins his acquisition of land along the length of Hadrian's Wall, including Housesteads in 1838, and in 1848 excavates Milecastle 42 and the Wall along Cawfields Crags.

1849
First Pilgrimage to Hadrian's Wall by the Society of Antiquaries of Newcastle upon Tyne.

1850–8
Clayton excavates at Housesteads.

1852–4
MacLauchlan plans forts along the length of the Wall.

1853–7
Clayton excavates Milecastle 37 (Housesteads), Milecastle 39 (Castle Nick) and the Wall between the fort and the Knag Burn gateway.

1863
Dr Bruce publishes his *Handbook to the Roman Wall*.

1866
1st Edition Ordnance Survey 6-inch map published covering middle lengths of Hadrian's Wall (sheet LXXXIII).

1883
Further excavations at Housesteads under Clayton.

1898
Housesteads' interior extensively trenched and the overall plan of the fort established by Bosanquet.

The twentieth century

From 1907 archaeological research on Hadrian's Wall became dominated by the universities of Durham and, later, Newcastle upon Tyne. Conservation grew increasingly important and the 1930s saw threats to the Wall from development. These were countered by the donation of Housesteads and much of the Wall to the National Trust. In 1987 Hadrian's Wall was declared a World Heritage Site by UNESCO and is today visited by as many as 500,000 people every year.

1907–12
J. P. Gibson and F. G. Simpson excavate Haltwhistle Burn Roman Fortlet. Simpson continues to repair the Wall and excavates Milecastle 39, as well as Turrets 36a, 37a, 38a, 39a and 41b, as well as a peel tower above Peel Gap.

1925
Durham University Excavation Committee carry out excavations at Great Chesters.

1929
The Chesters estate is sold.

1930
Housesteads Fort and the Wall between Milecastle 37 and the Knag Burn gateway donated to the National Trust.

1931–2
Excavations at Housesteads conducted by the National Trust.

1933–7
Excavations by the Department of Archaeology of Durham University under Eric Birley, including milecastles 37 and 38 and the Knag Burn gateway. Milking Gap settlement excavated by Kilbride-Jones.

1945
Turret 36b at Housesteads excavated by Richmond and Simpson.

1951
Housesteads Fort placed under guardianship of Ministry of Works.

1954–73
Excavations at Housesteads by Smith, Wilkes and Charlesworth revealing the *principia* (1954), *praetorium* (1967–9), the south-east angle and latrines (1968), barrack blocks (1969–71) and the hospital (1969–73).

1974–81
Department of Archaeology at Newcastle University hold annual training excavations at Housesteads.
Barrack XIII, rampart back areas 20–21 excavated by Daniels, Gillam and Crow.

1982–9
Excavations along the line of the Wall carried out by the National Trust under direction of Crow.

1984–5
Roman temporary camps on Cawfields Common surveyed by RCHME.

1985–7
Excavation and consolidation at Milecastle 39 and on the line of the Wall on Mons Fabricius and Sycamore Gap.

1986
RCHME survey of Housesteads Fort, *vicus* and environs.

1986–8
Excavations along the line of the Wall through Peel Gap, additional tower discovered.

1987
Hadrian's Wall declared a World Heritage Site by UNESCO.

1987–91
RCHME Hadrian's Wall Linear Survey.

1990–1
Detailed survey at 1:1000 of the National Trust 'old' estate conducted by Crow and Lofthouse.

1994
Hadrian's Wall National Trail announced.

1996
Hadrian's Wall Management Plan published by English Heritage outlining the future management proposals for the entire length of the Wall.

REFERENCES

BEDE (ed. and trans. B. Colgrave and R. A. B. Mynors) 1969. *Ecclesiastical History of the English People*. London

BIDWELL, P. T. and WATSON, M. 1996. 'Excavations on Hadrian's Wall at Denton, Newcastle upon Tyne', *Archaeol Aeliana* 5, 24, 1–56

BIRLEY, E. 1937–8. 'A modern building at Housesteads', *Proc Soc Antiq Newcastle upon Tyne* 4, 8, 191–3

1961. *Research on Hadrian's Wall*, Kendal

1962. 'Sir John Clark's visit to the north of England in 1724', *Durham Univ J Archaeol* 12, 221–46

BIRLEY, E., CHARLTON, J. and HEDLEY, P. 1933. 'Excavations at Housesteads in 1932', *Archaeol Aeliana* 4, 10, 82–96

BIRLEY, E. and KEENEY, R. 1935. 'Fourth report on excavations at Housesteads', *Archaeol Aeliana* 4, 12, 204–59

BIRLEY, E., KEENEY, G. S., SIMPSON, F. G., STEER, K. E. and RICHMOND, I. A. 1936. 'Milecastles along Hadrian'sWall explored in 1935–6', *Archaeol Aeliana* 4, 13, 261–75

BLAIR, H. 1934. 'Housesteads Milecastle', *Archaeol Aeliana* 4, 11

BOSANQUET, R. C. 1904. 'Excavations along the line of the Roman Wall in Northumberland. 1: The Roman camp at Housesteads', *Archaeol Aeliana* 2, 25, 193–300

1929. 'Dr John Lingard's notes on the Roman Wall', *Archaeol Aeliana* 4, 6, 130–62

BOSANQUET, R. C. and BIRLEY, E. 1955. 'Robert Smith and the observations upon the Picts Wall (1707–9)', *Trans Cumberland Westmorland Antiq Archaeol Soc* 2, 55, 154–71

BRAND, J. 1789. *The History and Antiquities of the Town and County of Newcastle upon Tyne*, Vol. I, London

BREEZE, D. and DOBSON, B. 1987. *Hadrian's Wall*, 3rd edn, London

BRUCE, J. C. 1851 *The Roman Wall*, 1st edn, London and Newcastle upon Tyne

1863. *A Wallet Book of Hadrian's Wall*, 1st edn, London and Newcastle upon Tyne

1867. *The Roman Wall*, 2nd edn, London and Newcastle upon Tyne

1881. *Handbook to the Roman Wall*, 2nd edn, London and Newcastle upon Tyne

1921. *Handbook to the Roman Wall*, 8th edn, London and Newcastle upon Tyne

BUCKLEY, S. 1972. 'The geology of the Housesteads area'. Unpublished dissertation, University of Newcastle upon Tyne

BUDGE, G. 1903. *An Account of the Roman Antiquities Preserved in the Museum at Chesters, Northumberland*, London

BURGESS, C. 1984. 'The prehistoric settlement of Northumberland: A speculative survey', in R. Micket and C. Burgess (eds) 1984, 126–75

CAMDEN, W. 1722. *Britannia* (ed E. Gibson), London

CHARLESWORTH, D. 1968. 'Recent work on Hadrian's Wall', *Archaeol Aeliana* 4, 46, 68–74

CLAYTON, J. 1855a. 'Account of excavations at the Mile Castle of Cawfields on the Roman Wall', *Archaeol Aeliana* 1, 6, 54–9

1855b. 'Notes on the disinterment of the Mile Castle immediately west of the Roman Station of Borcovicius', *Archaeol Aeliana* 1, 6, 269–76

COLLINGWOOD, R. G. 1931. 'Ten years' work on Hadrian's Wall, 1920–1930', *Trans Cumberland Westmorland Antiq Archaeol Soc* 31, 87–110

COLLINGWOOD, R. G. and WRIGHT R. P. 1965. *The Roman Inscriptions of Britain*, Vol. I, Oxford

CROW, J. G. 1988. 'An excavation of the north curtain wall of Housesteads', *Archaeol Aeliana* **5**, 16, 61–124

1989. 'Construction and reconstruction in the central sector of Hadrian's Wall', in V. A. Maxfield and M. J. Dobson (eds) 1989, 44–7

1991. 'A review of current research on the turrets and curtain of Hadrian's Wall', *Britannia* **22**, 44–7

1995. *Housesteads*, London

CROW, J. G. and JACKSON, M. 1997. 'The excavation of Hadrian's Wall at Sewingshields and the discovery of a long cist burial', *Archaeol Aeliana* **5**, 25, 61–8

DANIELS, C. M. 1989. *The Eleventh Pilgrimage of Hadrian's Wall*, Newcastle upon Tyne

DARK, K. R. 1992. 'A sub-Roman redefence of Hadrian's Wall?', *Britannia* **23**, 111–21

DARK, K. R. and DARK, S. P. 1996. 'New archaeological and palynological evidence for a sub-Roman reoccupation of Hadrian's Wall', *Archaeol Aeliana* **5**, 24, 57–72

DORNIER, A. 1968. 'Knag Burn, Housesteads, Northumberland', *Archaeol Newsbull Northumberland, Cumberland and Westmorland* **1** (Jan 1968), 2–4

1969. 'Knag Burn, Housesteads, Northumberland', *Archaeol Newsbull Northumberland, Cumberland and Westmorland* **1** (Jan 1969), 5

FITCH, F. J. and MILLER, J. A. 1967. 'The age of the Whin Sill', *Geological Journal* **5**, 233–50

FORTLEY, R. 1993. *The Hidden Landscape. A Journey into the Geological Past*, Pimlico

FOWLER, P. 1983. *The Prehistory of Farming*, Cambridge

FRASER, G. M. 1971. *The Steel Bonnets*, London

FRERE, S. 1987. *Britannia – A History of Roman Britain*, 3rd edn, London

GIBSON, J. P. and SIMPSON, F. G. 1909. *The Roman Fort on the Haltwhistle Burn*, Newcastle upon Tyne

GILDAS (1978). *The Ruin of Britain and Other Works* (ed M. Winterbottom), Chichester

HAVERFIELD, F. and MACDONALD, G. 1924. *The Roman Occupation of Britain*, Oxford

HEDLEY, P. 1936. 'Medieval cultivation at Housesteads, Northumberland', *Proc Soc Antiq Newcastle upon Tyne* **6**, 306–8

HIGHAM, N. 1986. *The Northern Counties to 1000 AD*, London

1993. *The Kingdom of Northumberland 350–1100*, Stroud

HODGSON, J. 1822. 'Observations on the Roman Station at Housesteads', *Archaeol Aeliana* **1**, 1, 263–320

1828. *The History of Northumberland*, Part 3, Vol. II, Newcastle upon Tyne

1840. *The History of Northumberland*, Part 2, Vol. III, Newcastle upon Tyne

HORSLEY, J. 1732. *Britannia Romana*, London

HOSKINS, W. G. 1955. *The Making of the English Landscape*, London

HUNTER, C. 1702. (Letter in) *Phil Trans Roy Soc Lond* **23**, 278, 1131

HUTTON, W. 1802. *The History of the Roman Wall, which crosses the Island of Britain from the German Ocean to the Irish Sea, describing its ancient state and its appearance in the year 1801*, London

ILLUSTRATED LONDON NEWS 1930a. 'Crown of our chief Roman monument given to the Nation', 18 January, 84–5

1930b. 'Hadrian's Wall and quarrying in the threatened area', 26 April, 735; and 'Where quarrying menaces our chief Roman monument' (Reconstruction of Housesteads Fort), 26 April, 736–7

JOBEY, G. 1960. 'Some rectilinear settlements of the Roman period in Northumberland', *Archaeol Aeliana* **4**, 38, 1–39

1966. 'A note on "Sow Kilns"', *J Univ Newcastle upon Tyne Agric Soc* **20**, 2–3

JOHNSON, S. 1989. *Hadrian's Wall*, London

KILBRIDE-JONES, H. E. 1938. 'The excavation of a native settlement at Milking Gap, Highshield, Northumberland', *Archaeol Aeliana* **4**, 15, 305–50

LAWSON, W. 1966. 'The origins of the Military Road from Newcastle to Carlisle', *Archaeol Aeliana* **4**, 44, 185–207

LEE, W. 1876. *Historical Notes of Haydon Bridge and District*, Hexham

MACLAUCHLAN, H. 1857. *The Roman Wall and Illustrations of the Principal Vestiges of Roman Occupation in the North of England*, London

MAXFIELD, V. A and DOBSON, M.J (eds) 1989. *Roman Frontier Studies*, Exeter

MICKET, R. 1984. 'John Collingwood Bruce and the Roman Wall controversy: the formative years 1848–1858', in R. Micket and C. Burgess (eds) 1984, 243–63

MICKET, R. and BURGESS C. (eds) 1984. *Between and Beyond the Walls: Essays on the Prehistory and History of North Britain in Honour of George Jobey*, Edinburgh

MOORE, M.F. 1915. *The Lands of the Scottish Kings in England*, London

NORTH, R. 1742. *The Life of the Right Honorable Francis North, Baron of Guildford*, London

NRO. Northumberland Records Office

ORNSBY, G. (ed) 1878. 'Selections from the Household Books of Lord William Howard of Naworth Castle', *Surtees Soc* **68**

PEARSON, M.P. 1993. *Bronze Age Britain*, London

RACKHAM, O. 1986. *History of the Countryside*, London

RAISTRICK, A. 1973. *Industrial Archaeology*, London

RAMM, H.G., McDOWALL R.D.J. and MERCER, E. 1970. *Shielings and Bastles*, London

RICHMOND, I.A. 1944. 'Roman Britain in 1943', *J Rom Stud* **35**, 76–9

RIVET, A.L.F. and SMITH C. 1981. *The Place-Names of Roman Britain*, London

ROGAN, J. 1954. 'Christopher Hunter, antiquary and historian', *Archaeol Aeliana* **4**, 32, 116–26

RYDER, P. 1990. *Bastles and Towers in the Northumberland National Park*, Newcastle upon Tyne

SANDERSON, R.P. (ed) 1891. *Survey of the Debateable and Border Lands, taken in A.D. 1604*, Newcastle upon Tyne

SIMPSON, F.G. 1931. Note on the excavation in the North Gateway, in 'Roman Britain in 1930', *J Rom Stud* **21**, 218

SIMPSON, G. 1976. *Watermills and Military Works on Hadrian's Wall*, Kendal

SKINNER, J. 1978. *Hadrian's Wall in 1801. Observations on the Roman Wall by the Rev. John Skinner* (ed. H. Coombes and P. Coombes), Bath

SPAIN, G. 1921. 'The Black Dyke', *Archaeol Aeliana* **3**, 14, 121–68

STAMPER, P. 1989. *The Farmer Feeds Us All*, Shrewsbury

STOREY, T. 1973. *Haltwhistle and South Tynedale. An Introduction to the Geology, Industrial Archaeology and History of South-West Northumberland and the East Cumberland Border*, Haltwhistle

STUKELEY, W. 1776. *Itinerarium Curiosum*, Oxford

TAYLOR, C. 1975. *Fields in the English Landscape*, London

TEUTONICO, J.M., McCAIG, I., BURNS, C. and ASHURST, J. 1993. *The Smeaton Project: Factors Affecting the Properties of Lime-Based Mortars*, London

THIRSK, J. 1969. *The Agrarian History of England and Wales, Volume V (1500–1640)*, Cambridge

1975. *The Agrarian History of England and Wales, Volume VI (1640–1750)*, Cambridge

TOPPING, P. 1989. 'Early cultivation in Northumberland and the Borders', *Proc Prehist Soc* **55**, 161–79

WARBURTON 1753. *Vallum Romanum*

WATSON, G. 1970. *Goodwife Hot and Others. Northumberland's Past as shown in its Place Names*, Newcastle upon Tyne

WELFARE, A.T. 1986. 'The Greenlee Lough palimpsest; an interim report on the 1985 season', *Northern Archaeology* **7**, 2

WELFARE, H. and SWAN, V. 1995. *Roman Camps in Britain – The Field Archaeology*, RCHME

WHITAKER, H. 1950. *A Descriptive List of the Maps of Northumberland 1576–1900*, Newcastle upon Tyne

WHITWORTH, A. 1990. 'The Housesteads bastle', *Archaeol Aeliana* **5**, 13, 8

WRATHMELL, S. 1975. 'Deserted and shrunken villages of southern Northumberland'. Unpublished Ph.D thesis

WRIGHT, R.P. 1936. 'Excavations *Per Lineam Valli* in 1935', *Durham Univ J Archaeol* **28**, 339–46

INDEX